Interactive Press

Voyagers

Mark Pirie is a Wellington, New Zealand writer, editor, publisher and critic. From 1995-2005 he initiated, co-edited and produced the literary magazine **JAAM** *(Just Another Art Movement).*

His works include 21 books of poems, a book of song lyrics, and a book of short fiction. In 1998 he edited **The NeXt Wave** *anthology of New Zealand 'Generation X' writing. He currently edits the* **HeadworX New Poetry Series** *(http://headworx.eyesis.co.nz) and the poetry journal* **broadsheet**, *and co-organizes the Winter Readings series of events in Wellington.*

A verse novel, **Tom**, *will be published by Poets Group, Christchurch in 2009.*

Tim Jones is a poet, short story writer and novelist. His most recent books are the short story collection **Transported** *(Vintage, 2008), which was long-listed for the 2008 Frank O'Connor International Short Story Award; the poetry collection* **All Blacks' Kitchen Gardens** *(HeadworX, 2007); and the fantasy novel* **Anarya's Secret** *(RedBrick, 2007). More information: http://timjonesbooks.blogspot.com*

Interactive Press
The Literature Series

Mark Pirie

Tim Jones

Voyagers

Science Fiction Poetry
from New Zealand

edited by Mark Pirie and Tim Jones

Interactive Press
Brisbane

Interactive Press
an imprint of IP (Interactive Publications Pty Ltd)
Treetop Studio • 9 Kuhler Court
Carindale, Queensland, Australia 4152
sales@ipoz.biz
ipoz.biz/IP/IP.htm

First published by IP in 2009
Introduction, arrangement and selection © Mark Pirie and Tim Jones, 2009;
poems as acknowledged.

Printed in 11 pt Cochin on 12 pt Myriad Pro by Sunny Young Printing,
Taiwan.

National Library of Australia
Cataloguing-in-Publication data:

Title: Voyagers : a New Zealand science fiction poetry anthology /
                  Editors, Mark Pirie and Tim Jones.

ISBN: 9781921479212 (pbk.)

Notes: Includes index.

Subjects: Science fiction, New Zealand--Poetry.

Other Authors/Contributors:
                  Pirie, Mark, 1974-
                  Jones, Tim, 1959-

Dewey Number: NZ821.100993

Acknowledgements

Jacket Images: Spectral-Design (front cover); Clint Spencer (back cover)

Jacket Design: David Reiter

Mark Pirie Photo: Michael O' Leary (2009)

Tim Jones Photo: Sonali Mukherji (2007)

The editors thank Dr David Reiter at IP for taking on the project and for publishing this anthology, and his editors and designers such as Emily Brinkworth for their work on the book. Thanks to Mallinson Rendel publishers, Wellington, New Zealand, for their assistance with an earlier version of this book. Niel Wright, Original Books, helped with the permission for the Ruth Gilbert poem, Anna Hodge provided help with the Auckland University Press (AUP) permissions. The Alexander Turnbull Library staff provided assistance in tracking down the Louis Johnson manuscript poems, and thanks is given to Cecilia Johnson for their reproduction.

Rachel Bush's unpublished poem 'Voyagers' was originally written for John Rimmer who had been commissioned to compose a song to be sung by Year 9 students at the opening of Botany Downs Secondary College, Auckland, New Zealand, in 2004.

Thanks too to the poets or executors (and their publishers) who generously agreed to letting their work appear here and for foregoing royalties in this instance.

– Mark Pirie and Tim Jones

For permission to reprint the poems in this anthology, acknowledgement is made to the following:

Fleur Adcock: excerpts from 'Gas' and 'Last Song' from *Poems 1960-2000* (2000), Bloodaxe Books, UK, to the author. Raewyn Alexander: 'in the future when we grow new brains' to the author. Puri Alvarez: 'Saturn's Rings' to the author. Jenny Argante: 'Space Age Lover' to the author. Tony Beyer: 'Kron' from *Craccum*, Volume 49, Issue 21, 30 September 1975 to the author. Peter Bland: 'An Old Man and Science Fiction' revised from *Habitual Fevers* in *3 Poets: Peter Bland, John Boyd and Victor O'Leary* (1958), Capricorn Press to the author. Iain Britton: 'Departing Takaparawha' to the author. Alan Brunton: 'Vis Imaginitiva' from *Slow Passes: 1978-1988* (1991), Auckland University Press (AUP); and 'F/S' from *Ecstasy* (2001), Bumper Books, to the executor Michele Leggott. Dana Bryce: 'Dreams of Alien Love' from *Aliens and Lovers* (1983) ed. Millea Kenin, Unique Graphics, USA, to the author. Rachel Bush: 'Voyagers' to the author. Alistair Te Ariki Campbell: 'Looking at Kapiti' from *The Dark Lord of Savaiki: Collected Poems* (2005), Hazard Press to the author. Meg Campbell: 'The End of the World' from *The Better Part* (2000), Hazard Press to the executor Alistair Te Ariki Campbell. Gordon Challis: 'The Thermostatic Man' from *Building* (1963), Caxton Press to the author. Janet Charman: 'in your dreams' to the author. Mary Cresswell: 'Metastasis' to the author. James Dignan: 'Great Minds' to the author. John Dolan: 'In Which I Materialize, Horribly Maimed, in the Transporter Room of the *Enterprise*' from *Stuck Up: poems from Great Central Lake* (1995), AUP; and 'The Siege of Dunedin' from *People with Real Lives Don't Need landscapes* (2003), AUP to the author. Marilyn Duckworth: 'Thin Air' from *Other Lovers' Children* (1975), Pegasus Press to the author. David Eggleton: '60-Second Warning' from *People of the Land* (1988), Penguin Books (NZ) Ltd; and 'Overseasia' from *Rhyming Planet* (2001), Steele Roberts Ltd to the author. Chris Else: 'Hypnogogia' to the author. Andrew Fagan: 'A Spaceship Has Landed Near Nuhaka' from *Take the Chocolates and Run* (1984), David Cohen Publications to the author. A.R.D. Fairburn: '2000 A.D.' from *Collected Poems* (1966), Pegasus Press to the executor Dinah Holman. Cliff Fell: 'In Truth or Consequences' from *Beauty of the Badlands* (2008), Victoria University Press (VUP) to the author. Gary Forrester: 'The Thirst That Can Never Be Slaked' to the author. Janis Freegard: 'Beside the Laughing Kitchen' to the author. Robin Fry: 'Lift-off' from *Weather Report* (2001), Inkweed to the author. Ruth Gilbert: 'Still Centre' from *Selected Poems, 1941-1998* (2008), Original Books to the author. David Gregory: 'Einstein's Theory Simply Explained' to the author. Nic Hill: 'Somewhere Else' to the author. Kevin Ireland: 'Instructions About Global Warming' from *How to Survive the Morning* (2008), Cape Catley to the author. Rob Jackaman: excerpt from *Lee: A Science Fiction Poem* (1976), Underoak Press to the author. Anna Jackson: 'Death Star', from *The Pastoral Kitchen* (2001), AUP to the author. Louis Johnson: 'Four Poems from the Strontium Age' from *New Worlds for Old* (1957), Capricorn Press and *Selected Poems* (2000), VUP; 'Love Among the Daleks' from ATL, MS-Papers-8095-030; and 'To a Science-Fiction Writer' from ATL, MS-Papers-8095-017 to the executor Cecilia Johnson and the Alexander Turnbull Library, Wellington, New Zealand. Tim Jones: 'The stars, Natasha' from *Boat People* (2002), HeadworX; and 'Good Solid Work', 'The First Artist on Mars', and 'Touchdown' from *All Blacks' Kitchen Gardens* (2007), HeadworX to the author. David Kārena-Holmes: 'Your Being' from *From the Antipodes* (2002), Maungatua Press to the author. Phil Kawana: 'This machine kills aliens' from *Jewels in the Water* ed. Terry Locke (2000), Leaders Press, University of Waikato to the author. Fiona Kidman: 'An aftermath' from *Wakeful Nights: Selected Poems* (1991), Vintage/Random House to the author. Hilaire Kirkland: 'Three Poems' from *Blood Clear and Apple Red* (1981), Wai-te-ata Press to the executor Michael Neill. Katherine Liddy: 'Crab Nebula' from

AUP New Poets 3 (2008), AUP to the author. Rachel McAlpine: 'Satellites' from
Selected Poems (1988), Mallinson Rendel to the author. Tracie McBride: 'Contact' to the
author. Seán McMahon: 'planet one' from *Apocalyptic Bodies* (c.1994), self-published to
the author. Harvey McQueen: 'After the Disaster' from *Recessional* (2004), HeadworX;
and 'Return' from *broadsheet 2: new new zealand poetry* (2008), The Night Press to the
author. Owen Marshall: 'Awakening' from *Occasional: 50 Poems* (2004), Hazard Press
to the author. Jane Matheson: 'An Alien's Notes on first seeing a prunus-plum tree' to
the author. Thomas Mitchell: 'Rituals' to the author. Harvey Molloy: 'Nanosphere'
from *The White Album Readings* ed. Mark Pirie (2008), ESAW and *Moonshot* (2008),
Steele Roberts Ltd to the author. Michael Morrissey: 'UFOs in Autumn' from *Taking
in the View* (1986), AUP; and 'Are the Andromedans Like Us' from *The American Hero
Loosens His Tie* (1988), VanGuard Xpress to the author. James Norcliffe: 'the ascent'
from *Villon in Millerton* (2007), AUP to the author. Michael O'Leary: 'Hey man, Wow!
[Jimi Hendrix]' and 'Nuclear Family – A Fragment' from *Toku Tinihanga: Selected Poems
1982-2002* (2003), HeadworX to the author. Stephen Oliver: 'Manned Mission to the
Green Planet' from *Night of Warehouses: New and Selected Poems 1978-2000* (2001),
HeadworX; and 'Letter to an Astronomer' from *Either Side the Horizon* (2005), Titus
Books to the author. Jacqueline Crompton Ottaway: 'Black Hole' to the author. Alistair
Paterson: 'Time traveller' from *Summer on the Côte d'Azur* (2004), HeadworX to the
author. Jack Perkins: 'Out of Time' to the author. Chris Pigott: '"We're thinking of going
into space"' from *JAAM* 6 (1997), Wai-te ata Press to the author. Mark Pirie: 'Dan and
His Amazing Cat'; 'Liam Going' from *The Search: Poems & Stories* (2007), ESAW; and
'The Rescue Mission' to the author. Vivienne Plumb: 'Signs of Activity' and 'The Last
Day of the World' from *Nefarious* (2004), HeadworX to the author. Jenny Powell *with*
John Dolan: 'Note to the Aliens' from *Double Jointed* (2003), Inkweed to the authors.
Cath Randle: 'The Purple fantastic, feels like elastic, spangled and plastic ray gun' to the
author. Trevor Reeves: 'they're keeping tabs' from *Apple Salt* (1976), Caveman Press to
the author. Helen Rickerby: 'Tabloid Headlines' from *JAAM* 2 (1995), Wai-te-ata Press
to the author. Anna Rugis: 'the poetry of the future' to the author. Bill Sewell: 'Space &
Time', 'The World Catastrophe', 'The Imaginary Voyage' and 'Utopia' from *Solo Flight*
(1982), University of Otago Press to the executor Amanda Powell. Iain Sharp: 'Karen
Carpenter Calls Interplanetary Craft' from *Poetrymath* ed. Mark Pirie (2006), ESAW to
the author. Meliors Simms: 'Two Kinds of Time' to the author. Robert Sullivan: excerpts
from *Star Waka* (1999), AUP to the author. Brian Turner: 'Earth Star' from *Beyond*
(1992), John McIndoe to the author. Tze Ming Mok: 'Lament of the imperfect copy of
Ensign Harry Kim' to the author. Richard von Sturmer: excerpt from 'Mill Pond Poems'
from *Suchness: Zen Poetry and Prose* (2005), HeadworX to the author. Nelson Wattie:
'The Art of Translation' from *The White Album Readings* ed. Mark Pirie (2008), ESAW
to the author. Mike Webber: 'My Personal Universe' from *Warm Primates* (2003), self-
published to the author. Simon Williamson: 'Japan 2030' from *Storyteller: Poems 1988-
1999* (2002), HeadworX to the executors Rob and Dianne Williamson. Sue Wootton:
'the verdigris critic' from *Hourglass* (2005), Steele Roberts Ltd to the author.

CONTENTS

ALTERED STATES

ET

WHEN WORLDS COLLIDE

The Final Frontier

INTRODUCTION

1

Selecting poems for this anthology would have been much easier
if there was a universally-agreed definition of science fiction. But
there isn't. A conservative definition might be that science fiction
is that genre of literature which speculates about the effects of
changes to the universe we know, where those changes follow or
are extrapolated from known scientific principles.

This definition is inadequate – it would exclude a number of
poems in this anthology – but it makes some key points:

- Science fiction is a literature of change.

- It is often set in the future.

- Science fiction is counter-factual: the universe is changed in
  at least one respect from the universe as it was known to the
  writer.

- The changes in science fiction are extrapolations based on
  accepted or speculative scientific principles.

This is why some types of universe are excluded, such as
those of fantasy, where the changes are supernatural rather than
natural, or of magic realism and fabulation, where the changes
are not rationalised. In addition, we reluctantly had to exclude

many excellent poems which dealt with astronomy, or with the history of space exploration, but which lacked the crucial element of speculation.

But what riches remain! You'll find the 'traditional' concerns of science fiction here: aliens, space travel, time travel, the end of the world – and also concepts you may not previously have thought of as science fiction. Whether questioning, apocalyptic or playful, these are poems which shine the flashlight of science fiction on our universe, and relish the strange images which result.

In this way we have chosen to organise the sections using well-known movie titles as thematic and fun links, i.e. 'Back to the Future' (futuristic or time travel poems), 'Apocalypse Now' (apocalyptic visions), 'Altered States' (robots and other altered states of existence), 'ET' (extraterrestrial sightings), 'When Worlds Collide' (explorations of other planets and stars), and 'The Final Frontier' (space travel poems).

2

Now for a few historical comments on the contents and make-up of this anthology. It is possible to trace a lineage of SF themes in New Zealand poetry, dating back to the 19th century. But it is not clear whether particular writers and their 'schools' or groups ever intended to create a specific genre of New Zealand science fiction poetry. Whereas, in Britain, the New Apocalyptics (of the 1940s) and the 'Martian School' (of the late 1970s/early '80s) emerged, and poets like D.M. Thomas specialised in SF poetry at various times, this was not the case in New Zealand. It is more likely that groups like 'The Wellington Group' of poets of the 1950s, several of whose poems are included in this collection, were 'occasional' writers on SF themes.

New Zealand poets have included SF themes in individual collections, such as Louis Johnson, *New Worlds for Old* (1957), Bill Sewell, *Solo Flight* (1982), David Eggleton, *People of the Land* (1988), Robert Sullivan, *Star Waka* (1999), Alan Brunton, *Ecstasy* (2001) or Tim Jones, *Boat People* (2002) and *All Blacks' Kitchen Gardens* (2007). Other collections, like Owen Leeming's *Venus is Setting* (1972), Cilla McQueen's *Antigravity* (1984), Bill Manhire's

Milky Way Bar (1991) or David Eggleton's *Rhyming Planet* (2001), have shown an awareness of science fiction themes in their titles. Individual small presses too held that awareness, such as Merlene Young's Kosmick Studios (in the '70s) and Nigel Rowe's Martian Way Press (in the '80s), though they didn't publish science fiction poetry (the idea had probably come to them from pop culture).

Fleur Adcock's 'Gas' (from *High Tide in the Garden* (1971)), Rob Jackaman's *Lee: A Science Fiction Poem* (1976), and Bill Sewell's sequence in *Solo Flight* are notable examples of longer New Zealand science fiction poems; but they are notable for their rarity as well as their quality.

It's a truism of SF criticism that SF, even if it's set in the far future, is mainly about the present. The nuclear bomb and the new threat of a man-made apocalypse, the space race of the '60s and the 1969 moon landing, SF films and TV shows, popular music i.e. classic rock to current electronica, the increasingly secular nature of our society, the information age ... all have been reflected in New Zealand science fiction poetry. Some of the poems in this anthology were written long enough ago that their imagined future is now in the past; others lay out a speculative map of our future.

3

Due to permissions issues and lack of necessary funding for payments to authors, we have not been able to include all the poems we wished in this anthology. Instead this book is very much compiled on the cooperation and goodwill of the poets included (and/or their publishers/executors), and as we complete the compilation of this anthology, we are sure that further New Zealand science fiction poems have been and are being written.

Among poets not included whom we know to have made contributions to the genre are Bill Manhire ('The Selenologist' and 'The Next Thousand'), R.A.K. Mason ('Latter-day Geography Lesson'), and Cilla McQueen ('Anti gravity'). Others like Murray Edmond, Hone Tuwhare, Denis Glover, James K. Baxter, Keith Sinclair, Jack Ross, Bernard Gadd, F.W.N. Wright, Ian Wedde, John Gallas, J.C. Sturm, Kendrick Smithyman, Allen Curnow (writing both as himself and as Whim-Wham), C.K. Stead,

Australian-domiciled Douglas Stewart in *Rutherford* (1962), or more recently Albert Wendt in *The Book of the Black Star* (2002) and American-now-NZ-based Bryan Walpert have written SF pieces. This is a snapshot of the field, and the first such anthology we know of in New Zealand, and we hope that it won't be the last such snapshot. Overseas, there have been several anthologies such as Keith Allen Daniels' *2001: A Science Fiction Poetry Anthology* (Anamnesis Press, San Francisco, USA). We're sure there are others too well worth searching out.

Above all, we hope you find this book an entertaining and challenging selection that gives you a new perspective on New Zealand, on science fiction, and on the range and scope of New Zealand poetry.

– Mark Pirie and Tim Jones
Wellington, New Zealand
January 2009

BACK TO THE FUTURE

Anna Rugis

the poetry of the future

it'll all be like mine

but not for long

then people will get into
elaborate hand gestures instead
and there'll be no applause because
then that will mean something else

Louis Johnson

To a Science-Fiction Writer

Strange how those in your field have become
so uniform, now, in a bleak view of the future.
What happened to perfectibility? What became
of great-grandfather's dream of progress –
the race aspiring always towards improvement,
perhaps becoming fulfilled? It was this
festered for you, failed, showed the sickness –
Man, and not the machine. But then,
the hopeful ancestor's sights were blurred
by braided nobility and the cavalry charge
blinding him to the ultimate use of the engine.
He had not known of the Marne or the Somme,
the millions rotting in trenches, gasping
against the poison gas. Not known of harvests
rusting or dumped in the midst of famine;
not known of the wheels and gears unleashing
the greatest terrors ever on civilised Europe.
Your lot is aware that under every bomb
is a kind of perfection – machine-turned
steel that mirrors the hand and satisfies
touch quite impersonally. But beauty
stops there. In your apple, man is the maggot
who has not learned to live with abstraction
any more than the ancestor with his dream.
Efficiency is fire-power and obsolescence, and in
your dream of the future – which could be clean
and good – it becomes more clearly established,
the human is the component that must be replaced.

30/6/70

A.R.D. Fairburn

2000 A.D.

The normal population
Has been evacuated from the South Island, which has been given
    over to the tourist industry for purposes of hunting, shooting,
    boozing, mountaineering, fishing and fornication.

Rugby football having been discarded as much too tame,
Fighting with spring-knives has become the national game,
Carried on by a small class of specially-bred gladiators,
The rest of the public being bubble-gum-blowing spectators.

Votes for cows was carried some years ago by a show of feet;
Totalitarian democracy is now complete,
And the present Prime Minister, known to everyone as Jackie,
Is a ten-year-old steer from Taranaki.

His authority, and that of Bullamy's, is only nominal, all power being
    vested (along with the right of self-perpetuation)
In GENERAL OECUMENICAL DEVELOPMENT (INC.), a
    world with headquarters in Monte Carlo and branches through-
    out the Creation.

A complete monopoly of Radio, Television, News and Information
    Services, Education and Entertainment, including six selected
    sub-varieties of religious practice
Is operated on behalf of G.O.D. (INC.) by the New Zealand Broad-
    serving Cactus,
Which is situated on the Desert Road, plumb in the middle
Of the North Island, where the major administrative fiddle
Of the nation is conducted
In an ant-hill suitably constructed.

Poets and artists are heavily subsidised by the State, on strict condi-
    tion that their work shall be totally incomprehensible,
Because that which is incomprehensible cannot possibly be subver-
    sive, a working assumption that is eminently sensible.
The defence of the country is in the hands of G.O.D. (Inc.) and (for
    decorative effect) a standing army of 100,000 marching girls
    ('Don't shoot until you see the whites
Of their eyes,' counsels the Ministry of Tourism), along with (not to
    be out-done) 50,000 marching bodgies in gents' Hawaiian floral
    shirtings and shocking-pink tights.

Now therefore, although everything worth buying has become pro-
    gressively scarcer and dearer,
Lift up your voices in joyous celebration of the Second Millennium
    of the Christian Era.

Janet Charman

in your dreams

Transit passengers
who wish to refrain
from inhaling

may simply press the icon
you see below you
on your left screen now

apply the mask
that falls from the bulkhead
directly above

If you are
disembarking
inhale

a spray
from
the kete

as the language ministry
officials
pass among you

and you will notice
a slight change
in cabin pressure

which is the effect of
crossing
the language barrier

Ladies and Gentlemen
Girls and Boys,
thank you for flying Air Aotearoa

Bill Sewell

Utopia

nowhere is there
to be found such health
as in the city of the mind:

marble gleaming white
under a gentle sun
and men & women
in freshly laundered robes
walk up & down conversing

cooling refreshments are offered
from well-situated stalls
(courteously & without charge)
respect and not subservience
sways the nods & smiles –

not a rag to be seen
not a smear of excrement
on the paving:

all this projected from the mind
onto faraway places & faraway times
while here & now the world
wobbles on its axis:

the bickering the jostling
and the passing of coins
one system soiling after another
no salve yet concocted
to remedy these boils –

or disease beyond disease
spreading out of the mind
to a living relic who
meets a lesser breed of men
conversation monitored
by a vigilant bureaucracy
hoodlums roaming the streets
to prey upon the feeble
or everyone just too happy
to give a damn about anything

(an 18th century adventurer
found more to admire in horses):

nowhere is there
any health and the boils
keep on erupting.

Alistair Paterson

Time traveller

Somewhere
you're writing, putting words together
but because I can't see you doing it
                              I have to visualise, guess
make inventions, imagine as
in the behaviour of blue penguins
                              what's happening to you
that you're hidden by water…
or you're riding a bicycle where
                              afternoon is trees & the sun –
                                        summer is endless…

You inhabit
a distant, an imaginary country
you live on high hills far from the sea
                              you're a time traveller
moving through the dust of centuries –
who travels like that because
                              it's the way you see yourself
or because someone's imagined you there
in front of the Parthenon
                              a thousand years on –
                    at the sea's edge watching the sun…

You're writing
(uncomfortably) at a kitchen table
or you're kneeling by a stream
                                        looking into the water
you're working in a library
(to the sound of bells, a flight of music)
                                you're using the telephone
or as in a painting by Chagall, moving
through the powers
                – the impossible, unbelievable powers –
                                        of the mind…

And suddenly I recognise
it's a mystery:
the fall of leaves in autumn
                        clouds drifting across the sky
light across a footpath, a roadway
that you're a long way off
                        & driving away from me –
driving along a highway towards
something, somewhere neither of us
                                has ever heard of
                        or is likely to arrive at…

You telephone to say
you've discovered
there are places where
                              the sky is luminous, the moon dark
the sun moves west to east – backwards –
that you can't understand
                              why no one else seems to see it:
I tell you I believe you – which I do
because there's no reason not to
                              because belief gives shape to things
                              structures the world…

You write at the kitchen table
& I remember
how the weather follows you
                              – the clouds, the moon, the night –
that the trick isn't
to think logically, be reasonable
                              but to work in a place with windows
that's open to air & light:
when the day's over, to walk in the park
                              & look at the harbour –
                         at leaves, at trees & the sky…

David Gregory

Einstein's Theory Simply Explained

When I returned
I went to see myself,
still working on the motor of the thing.
We had a pleasant chat,
so startling.
We talked of time, Einstein and you.
Then I went out,
denounced the project
and bought the weapon.
Knowing how he sleeps,
I shall kill him in the night,
so he will not have you
again.

Jenny Powell with *John Dolan*

Note to the Aliens

To be fossilised is actually a long shot
and yet, in yesterday's assembly
two children showed fossilised shells.
They, of course, have the calcium advantage.
They pay for it in mobility though –
and the long wait to be pushed, sea for hilltop.

In the layers of time where would
you be?
Upper-middle at best. If that. If ever.
But if I get lucky, let me explain
the much repaired teeth: don't assume
this skull ranked high in my tribe.
We had conquered; dentists needed work;
cake was everywhere. Until dentists
became rare. You can tell from
the following layer; greater prevalence
of untreated dental decay.
– A more honest portrait, all in all.
We are pressed there to prove something else.
Even fossils can lie.

Raewyn Alexander

in the future when we grow new brains

old ideas will not fit
same as new cars with improved engines
we'll be streamlined too with sleek genes
part eggplant and olive oil
lick your arm and enjoy a salad in Greece

in the future when we learn to love completely
broken hearts will be a joke
same as how wooden spoked wheels are laughable
tears will be rare and set into jewellery
our past blue but tomorrow lipsticked kisses

in the future we shall choose how to die in style
death the new black
every clone and thought kept on silicon chips
rebirth as natural as a botox break
grief played out in theatres for the old fashioned

in the future we will look back at now and smile
the colours and aromas rejuvenated in theme parks
revisiting who you used to be
meet the beings that tomorrow is built on
here you are now in person reading every word

Alan Brunton

F/S

All of the sun's radiant debris passes through us
and neutrinos on a voyage through the universe
that lasts millions of years smash through us
and we don't even blink, it takes all our time
to live our lives. It's over.
The intergalactic beings talked about everywhere,
the reps of Planet X, have rendezvoused
with Earth to prepare us for the trip to Nowhere.
Not for the first time. They came before on
such a night as this, before the zero-zero era,
to meet the priests of a fungal cult
with whom they had been exchanging
inter-planetary emissions. That meeting
with those *Homos* in their cold catacomb
35,000 years ago was the birth of the sacred.
After that hot night, weird old ant-men
fanned out among the population in their rags,
lighting lamps of mammoth fat
that fluttered like matches do
when you take a shortcut through the gloom
and in the fuzzy beams drank blood
in their fury straight from the hearts
of wild animals; they ascended to galaxies
you can only see from ladders,
other worlds with fragrant pastures.
Survivors of the cult contacted me personally
in September, 1987. They clutched me
though we were strangers – You have come back,
they wept, for another night of mushrooms!
Somewhere between Bordeaux and Paris.
There will be fragrant pastures, they cried,
and nights with you
on the journey to the Fourth Age.

Harvey Molloy

Nanosphere

The Enemy of the World
watery eyed, unkempt,
finally captured after months in a hole.

A lab coat prods his back dentures
with a disposable spatula. How
slow and compliant the prisoner moves
like a rest home inmate.

In this cosmos his capture
shall be eclipsed by news
of the accidental discovery of the end of time

as weightless above this earth
from the station console
Irina checks the Doppler shifts
from the Sombrero, Andromeda, closer Tau Ceti.

Aware of the pressure of the moment
she pauses to gaze at the withered fingers
of a passing river delta
then tells Control her final confirmation:

the expansion is over and the big crunch has begun
the slow seven billion year retrenchment
from universe to nanosphere.

Her news crosses the twittering
of the only known radio intelligence:

0800 chatline numbers
psychic advice lines
impending Serbian elections
weather updates
body counts
Chinese operas
Marilyn's slow turn in a hall of mirrors
Chico & the Man.

The day's journeying calls roll out
within the bounded horizon of a vast contracting dot.
There is only so much time. And time is running back.

The children watch television in the dark.

Meliors Simms

Two Kinds of Time

In some universes
time is experienced as linear.
Individuals move through their lives
cutting a track into their possibilities
and paving it into permanence behind them.
Aware only of the winding road they have chosen,
looking backwards down the line from now to birth
looking forward into the obscure thicket of the future
sometimes, peripherally aware of a bare hint
of what if's as what isn't.

In some universes
time is experienced as a plane.
Beings move around their existence
as an intimate landscape
treading and retreading every possibility.
Learning their lives as a farmer learns her land,
choosing every choice
exploring every opening,
until through preference
a rut is worn in the familiar
a dwelling in just one favourite moment or cycle of moments
a resting place from their endless wanderings.

When you sleep
these universes meet in your dreams.
Time leaks across the boundaries
so you can know a little
of the strange ways of linearity or planearity;
whichever is most unfamiliar to you.

Jack Perkins

Out of Time

A long time ago
in another dimension,
there wasn't enough time
to let the future happen
at normal speed.

So everything kept happening
faster and faster until all
the future was nearly
happening at once.

Imagine living a lifetime
in a split second
no wonder there was a big
BANG

When everything did happen at once.

In no time, the future exploded
creating our universe
and it's taking time
to space things out,
14 billion years so far.

Trouble is,
my birthdays
keep getting
closer together.

Jacqueline Crompton Ottaway

Black Hole

Massive objects distort
          space and time
weighty problems obscure
          the present moment
time coordinate t is infinity
wind rustles the trees

She hovers on the brink
          of a frozen star
horizons are sitting still
the singularity lies in her
future
there's no way she can
avoid it

Tim Jones

Good Solid Work

We'll laugh at this world one day.
It was all a simulation, we'll say –
nodding our virtual heads
smiling our virtual smiles –
why didn't we spot it before?
Nature could never
have come up with the emu
and the hammerhead shark was clearly a clue.

We talk without moving our lips, mind to mind.
Quantum theory's the clincher.
Don't sweat the small stuff, so those in charge
left the edges fuzzy
let the smallest particles
roam where they may.

Still, they did some things well –
the roots that riddled the ground
the rush of wind in the pines
the pressure of our children's hands.
Good work, we'll say, good solid work
nodding our virtual heads
smiling our virtual smiles
turning our eager faces to the soft electron rain.

Apocalypse Now

John Dolan

The Siege of Dunedin

Katyushka volley from a launcher on the Hocken
Arcs out toward their lines
On the black slope of Cargill.
They always answer
Promptly. Fireworks tonight –
Another free performance of interactive,
Monumental art.
The city lives for these late shows,
Red and green tracers lacing
Christmas stitches on the slopes. Every
Random horror makes Dunedin
More beautiful – the black djinns of smoke
Rising from what was once Barnett's,
Hit last week, still burning. Somewhere
On the back slope of Roslyn, a villa
Has become this fine black scarf
Tossed over the city's shoulder.

And love, love has come at last
To the dank alleys of Dunedin.
Love is everywhere: the big clouds
Sink gently like a penguin female
To meet the pillars of smoke. Birth-rates rise
To meet the casualty climb; we sing more
And drink less. Lonely crones smile
Every time a shell seeks them.
Couples filling sandbags on the Brighton trenches
Mate and marry
Overnight. The gulls hurry
Along like couriers, urged
By the warming wind. It gets so hot
In a city besieged! Dunedin

Was cold – we struggle to remember
That now. Everyone inside the perimeter
Is warm and quick, roaring out
'Stand by Me,' that song the All Blacks sang
In Gore's last desperate week.

No one needs beer or rugby now;
Enough for us the songs, the coupling
In rubble, and the pillars of smoke –
So beautiful! Half-mile-high
Battleflags, billowed in the wind!

David Eggleton

Overseasia

The soldiers of fortune now gathering
at Tropical Motel, President Drive, Boot Hill,
have been denounced as war criminals
by the new manager of the Buddhist
Ice Cream Parlour, whose FRO-ZEN
is a bestseller amongst steroid dealers.

Seizing on Inuit intuition,
venture capitalists, phoning in the performance,
invest aggressively in a fiscal epic
of titanic whale blubber futures, primed to go ape
and eating away at global nose cartilage,
on a journey to a satellite in meltdown.

El Niño's swoosh mark caresses islands,
squeezes Scud missiles out of Africa,
vaporises a trillionaire,
before coming to rest on internet's home-page
for fertility drug octuplets and fetal abuse survivors,
The Spermicide Girls: Posy Rash and friends.

In the City of the Plastic Tits,
in the Suburb of Golden Pompadours,
as fluorocarbons mist the atmosphere,
Joggers of the Apocalypse don't turn a hair,
when a bulging breastduct drips
on shimmering haystacks of milkshake straws.

Beneath Milan Station's vaulting cupola,
with glossy endorsement by the blushing parquetry,
Ebola models a straitjacket by Versace,
lately ascended to Heaven, a beatific surf Nazi,
pursued by a flying wedge of paparazzi,
who, falling, splinter the fine inlaid marquetry.

Fruitbat terrorist CHE Guava's bloody fist-print,
glue-fumed, laser-fixed, bar-coded, is logo'd
onto the collectable plastic carrier bags
of all respectable blood banks,
as, while splatter fests flex their can't-resist muscle,
Healthcares greet the new Lord of the Corpuscle.

Alistair Te Ariki Campbell

Looking at Kapiti

Sleep, Leviathan, shouldering the Asian
Night sombre with fear, kindled by one star
Smouldering through fog, while the goaded ocean
Recalls the fury of Te Rauparaha.

Massive, remote, familiar, hung with spray,
You seem to guard our coast, sanctuary
To our lost faith, as if against the day
Invisible danger drifts across the sea.

And yet in the growing darkness you lose
Your friendly contours, taking on the shape
Of the destroyer – dread Moby Dick whose
Domain is the mind, uncharted, without hope.

Without hope, I watch the dark envelop
You and like a light on a foundering ship's
Masthead the star go out, while shoreward gallop
The Four Horsemen of the Apocalypse.

Bill Sewell

The World Catastrophe

when the clouds began to
gather on the seventh day
the people knew a tremendous
thunderstorm was on the way
so they hurried (and why not?)
under cover till it was over

when the water edged up
to their necks on the tops
of the highest mountains
they knew there was a future
for aquatic creatures only –

all this came to pass
in the days before rainbows:

but what signs to expect
when fever sweeps the world
swollen glands & putrid boils
corpses heaped on wagons
rats slithering everywhere
and a muffled bell tolling?

when huge metallic spiders
stride across the land
over pub & church & corner-shop
incinerating in an instant
all that's organic & in motion?

when the trees revolt at last
pull themselves up by the roots
and advance (a camouflaged army)
out of their parks & squares
to hoist us up with their branches?

and the self-inflicted wound:
a cowboy astride a falling drum
the possibility *so long sustained*
that men can even bear it:
on the vast illuminated map
the moving dots move closer:

no rainbow but a monstrous cloud
accumulating into space
the fountains of the deep
and *the windows of heaven*
fouled & dusted forever –

(yet even now a ball of fire
may be quietly altering course
to cut across earth's orbit).

Rachel McAlpine

Satellites

I've been thinking about the migraine
as a game of Space Invaders,
or something jazzier, say Phoenix or Galaxians.
Mission: destroy all aliens, no matter how cute.

Those lights on the angular move
through tunnel vision,
that droop in the energy level and that sense
of stumbling, and all that jagged prettiness
lasering in on you alone,
a social worry in a secret club.

And nothing beats the migraine psyche
when your finger's on the button:
you push and push for a better score
and when you hit the top, you're so
ashamed, it's just not good enough.

Four thousand four hundred
satellites
are slung around the earth.
It's now official: over the rainbow
there's a lot of military stuff.
Now wouldn't that give you a headache?

The city's electric profile waits
for bombs to turn into birds
who will bomb the beautiful skyline.
We're all set up to invade
ourselves from space.

We who suffer love the drama.
We wouldn't give it up for health or peace.
And think what we've achieved –
how nearly perfect we've become
before the twenty-cent bits run out
and the game is over.

David Eggleton

60-Second Warning

The President pops one off
and the Pacific goes nuclear,
you cannot sound the all-clear,
you must obey this nightmare.
Hot flash, cold sweat, no, no, not yet.
The hottest holiday you've ever had.
Executives execute their orders,
a cryptic message from a birth controller.
No time for a funeral director,
no time for a quality coffin,
vaporised as you walk the dog,
incinerated as you saw that log.
Quick exit for a tormented teenager,
final curtain for a Frank Sinatra impersonator.
Red Alert. Reject. Danger. Danger.
King Kong is pounding on his tits
as the world gets blown to bits.
The Girl From Ipanema meets the Man From Rio
for one last samba beneath the sun.
It cost a bomb for that plutonium blonde.
Televise that face, watch this space.
Scrape the skin off the walls.
Phenomenal! Phenomenal!
Radioactive Tahitian miss,
on the face of it she's hit, she's hit.
Moruroa you evil genius,
your hell's teeth mouth spews fried fluorescent fish.
A love song turns to a hate story,
all God's children in the car park are bound for Glory.
Go-getter grannies shoot up an atomic brew.

Chain-smoking, chain-reaction existentialists cease to exist.
A home computer terminal spells zeros;
there are no nuclear holocaust heroes.
On another planet,
across a universe of voids,
are the megaton ruins of the Aucklandoids.
O, it is I, Neutronhead.
O, it is they, the dehumanised dead.
Major Accident and General Emergency,
like some mistake of the brain,
dance on the graves of the Kids from Fame
in a South Island Landscape Still Life with Acid Rain.
Angels turn to angel dust,
baby rainbows burst.
Close to home and closing in,
the impossible dream is doing its worst.

Meg Campbell

The End of the World

The shining cuckoo sings,
'It will surely be like this.
Just an ordinary day
suddenly turned nasty.
Grey sky and an oily sea.
The sun will suddenly move
in a crazy fashion.
       You won't
believe your eyes. But, then,
free falling you'll die
without a murmur.
       *The end
of the world is brief,'* sings
the bird in its whoops-a-daisy
voice. It has gone.
We think we hear it singing
from a distant tree.
       Since when
have birds the gift of prophecy?

Vivienne Plumb

The Last Day of the World

That will be the day none of the eggs will cook. There will be strange phenomena. Babies born with three ears. White elephants. Stains will appear on the wall. The heavens will open at midday and the rain will rattle down upon us. Ants will act like individuals. At home, the mail will never arrive. The silver beet and parsley will run to seed in twenty-four hours, and the stove will not light. Everything that insurance policies refuse to cover, will happen. The clock hands will move in reverse. The horrors will come upon us. Burning fires and a smell like five hundred sliced durians will prevail. There will be the sound of great flapping wings. The porridge will go bad. Chasms will slide open. We will never speak to each other again. It will be dark and our old lives will be nothing but a disappearing pinprick of light on the road ahead.

Louis Johnson

Four Poems From the Strontium Age

1.

Before the Day of Wrath

There were cities here in the hills
In my great-grandfather's youth
Where now are only blackened bricks and walls
Devoured in the year of wrath.

And in the desert where none of us
Dare venture, hearing tell
Of fabulous, dangerous monsters, flowers
Were said to emerge when rare rain fell.

Today the rain draws blood; the winds
Burn out our eyes; the barbarous
Plants tear flesh that never mends:
Sweet water-holes turn suddenly poisonous.

It must have been a lovely country once,
Populous and inventive – a golden age
Wherein the young knew laughter, loved to dance
Even grew old. Daylight as bright as courage

Existed for many hours at a time, we're told.
But these, perhaps, are fables meant to inspire
Us now in the darkness helping us to hold
Something to cherish crouched by the guttering fire.

2.

It's An Ill Wind …

There was a time when the patterns did not change
So frequently, so our instructor says.
In those days a girl would have thought it strange
To have two or three heads, to praise
Her lover's thirty-nine fingers with all her tongues,
And her narrow chest contained one set of lungs.

But how strange that would be to one of our modern youths
Who can pick out a girl with a breast for each of his mouths.

3.

Spring

All day the black rain has fallen
And now, in the hour of light
The livid river and the lake are swollen;
The range of hills that were bright

And red with their carpet of dust
Are dissolving away. Soon there will be
No shelter: again we must
Pack and move in search of kinder country.

Then will begin again that dread migration
Through sightless deserts, and the silent land
Reflecting sickness into our eyes, starvation
Bloating the children with its grotesque hand.

And never knowing which way is the best
To set the foot because the perils met there
Can never be foreseen nor wholly guessed,
For who can tell what colour of the air

Harbours most pain? Surely the Spring
Is the most bitter season of suffering.

4.

Haven

We have come to a quiet valley in the hills
Where a road, this time unbroken, runs
Right back to the desert fringe. It fills
Us with a dreaming hope. The sun's

Mild light is clean; about and above
The slopes are grassy. In our ears
The little river sings a song like love.
In the old country, for two thousand years

There ruled a king called God, the story goes.
It seems impossible, but here is a place
Where one might trust to fable. Flowers grow
And trees stand straight beside the watercourse.

Let us not be afraid. After two days and nights
In such a haven, we fear that we may have brought
With us those breeding poisons of the world's blight
That will blacken the earth here and pollute the light.

And already the leaders confer in the common interest,
And it's rumoured that they plan to eliminate
The sickliest and those of us who are least
Like men should be. Oh, may we all grow straight

In this place of the sun. Let me not think of these
Cruel facts of life in this valley of green trees.

Michael O'Leary

Nuclear Family – A Fragment

In dreams I walked
    Through crowded, confused streets
    Where people, scurrying like rats
                on a sinking ship
    Ran in all directions towards survival

In dreams I moved
    Through a human fog
    It was my single purpose
    That kept me going, and
    Kept me from going insane,
    To find you and the child whom I love

When I saw you in the hall of mirrors
    Like all the other victims
              you radiated decay
    Your hair had shrivelled and gone grey overnight
    I held my arms outstretched
    Hoping you and your child would embrace me
    But you turned away
              and she ran to you, as if I were
                    a stranger

I picked up my gun
    And went outside where things weren't quite
              so grim
(I mean this war has killed love
    so what's a pile of rotting bodies)
In my uniform, I watched the beauty of
              another atomic flash
    A tank drove by
        I jumped aboard
        And we headed toward
    The war which can never be won!

Ruth Gilbert

Still Centre

45

Noon turned to night;
Atomic-voiced
The thunder mushroomed overhead,
Windows and mirrors screamed with light,
But placidly she went on kneading bread:
'A chimney down, or maybe two,' she said.

Fleur Adcock

Last Song

Goodbye, sweet symmetry. Goodbye, sweet world
of mirror-images and matching halves,
where animals have usually four legs
and people nearly always two;
where birds and bats and butterflies and bees
have balanced wings, and even flies
can fly straight if they try. Goodbye
to one-a-side for eyes and ears and arms
and breasts and balls and shoulder-blades
and hands; goodbye to the straight line
drawn down the central spine,
making us double in a world
where oddness is acceptable only
under the sea, for the lopsided lobster,
the wonky oyster, the creepily rotated
flatfish with both eyes over one gill;
goodbye to the sweet certitudes of our
mammalian order, where to be
born with one eye or three thumbs
points to not being human. It will come.

In the next world, when this one's gone skew-whiff,
we shall be algae or lichen, things
we've hardly even needed to pronounce.
If the flounder still exists it will be king.

Rob Jackaman

from **Lee: A Science Fiction Poem**

4. Viaticum

'I dreamed I saw St. Augustine
Alive as you or me,
Moving through these quarters
In the utmost misery…'
– Bob Dylan, 'I Dreamed I Saw St. Augustine'

Though it was true
Sometimes the radiation
Sickness hung in pockets
In the mountains where he worked
Nothing halted his task
Of reconstructing the past
On the evidence available.
And his collection grew:
Miraculously
       saved
An empty bottle a tin can
Jagged and bleeding
With rust   the coil
Of a small motor –
In general the cogs and springs
That make a world
Tick.
      Lost
In the
    past   passing
For a living man and all the while
A corpse, and another week
Gone   another
Week further away

From the past
          (groping for…)
Though I can see the towns
Are hungry   how
The buildings are thin and grey
And I see
          windows with the light
Glinting blankly in them
                    (may they be washed clean)
And empty auditoriums
Littered with remains,
And the air vents on the sky –
Scrapers sniffing for clean air
And the drains like mouths
Grinning in the gutters
                    (may all these too
Be purified)
With a film of oil
Over the lips, and my hands and feet
Throbbing in the heat,
And hurrying to be on time but
              Too late
                    too late
too late
          too late too late
And he woke up, and it was time
To start searching again.

Yellow ochre
Cliffs of clay
Etched by the storms
Into strange shapes
Like slaves
          rising from the earth,
Salt pans where an estuary had boiled
Dry, flat shallows
With floating scum and weird
Spiked plants scattered
                    and reflections

Of dark birds in the air, and
Sticky water
                over the eyes and
Thirst.

So it must have been
In the beginning
After the first creation
When   things
Hatched, and the pterodactyl
Was the word.

So it was now   with Lee
In his mind   wandering
A martyr in the sand;
                        with wind
Singing like choirs
Of Hollywood trebles in the wings
For the show
                down he came
Over a ridge and there
Like Lazarus
                rising above
Dead rock
                a building (in the old style
Called sky-scraper, a column of a
Million pigeon-holes
For housing all the souls
That teem in the city);
And upward it reared
Into the heavens
And the sky opened for it and
A light shone out
And then,
            voice breaking through
The silence

            The bomb fell.

Marilyn Duckworth

Thin Air

Gulping thin air of an ecological nightmare –
Animals mutated, the children screaming –
She woke to the pandemonium of a still house.
Alone now, she kicked the stiff mechanism of reassurance.
Go back to sleep – it was only a nasty dream.
Too late.

She already knew the dream was certainly real.
Not here, not now, but somewhere, some day,
She would pick up her feet among the red insects,
Carrying her children high on breaking shoulders,
Trembling before the poisonous distance to safety,
Murmuring in their little lemon coloured ears
The reassurances she could not now, or ever
Give to herself.

Fiona Kidman

An aftermath

for J.M. Coetzee

The nightmare of the flood
had left the landscape pockmarked
and blue like the moon and then
the looting began and the man
wearing round spectacles made of smoke
coloured non-reflective
glass walked over the pitted
world with the woman with red
hair that would have shone in the sun
if there had been any left, shooting
the looters. Angry dogs, savage
and at loose, sprang at the couple
of the man with the shaded eyes handed
his pistol to the woman with red
hair, instructing her to shoot the animals.
When they came to me he handed
me the pistol and instructed
me to shoot the woman
in the stomach. The red strands and the blue
clay were mixed on the surface of the earth
and it was quite clearly my fault, though
it seemed I would be allowed
to go without questioning.

Kevin Ireland

Instructions About Global Warming

for Michael Sharkey

It all began when I suggested that
it could be useful to talk about the weather.
It seemed to me to be a harmless issue.
It could not possibly disturb our friendships,
our businesses could continue as normal
and members of friendly communities
would be able to join in the discussion
without first looking under their beds.

Yet the subject turned out to be
not quite what it might have been.
Nearly everyone was of the same mind
only on this one point. So it seemed politic
to me that we should take a long break
to see whether we could sort out some
of the minor disagreements and put a stop
to the anguish, mutterings and threats …

When we returned I considered it sensible
to wear body armour and a steel helmet,
and to carry a riot shield. I also had to insist
on being addressed as Sir. Someone
had to take charge, for my audience seemed
to have a touch of sunstroke. It was expedient
to station guards with guns around the hall
to protect sanity and the water supply.

The climate was a neutral subject, but if people
are now going to have to be cast out to die
for answering back about cloud formations,
temperatures, gales and droughts, we must regard it
as nature's way of sorting out the competition.
They ought to try not to be so damned selfish.
There are variables in the sky that they are soon
going to have to sign up to once and for all.

Altered States

Iain Sharp

Karen Carpenter Calls Interplanetary Craft

Extinction nigh, desperate for warmth,
the fuel-starved bodies of anorexics
sprout hair brow to toe as a makeshift blanket.

Karen clasps her furry digits and beams
a final telepathic telegram
to cosmic rovers. Somewhere organisms

must thrive outside the food chain, free from grub
and shit, enduring for centuries, perhaps
forever, and thus free from hormonal surges,

free to say goodbye to love, except the kind
of sibling fondness Karen feels for Richard,
but without the prickles, without the need

to let Richard doodle elephantine
overtures (lest he fume or cry) before
Karen's silky alto cuts to the quick.

Once she wished for an alien rescuer
like Michael Rennie as Klaatu in *The Day
The Earth Stood Still* – all brylcreemed aquiline

superiority in his sexy lurex
jumpsuit. But she's gone beyond such aching,
beyond panic, beyond rescue. She'd just like to hope

someone in the universe has got it right –
hairless, smooth, no mess, no odour, empowered
joule by joule direct from a benign sun.

Gordon Challis

The Thermostatic Man

The world could fall to pieces any moment now; with luck it won't,
mainly because it hasn't yet. Though cracks appear, I'll merely count
them leeway spaces left so masses may expand to meet and don't.

But I, who used to walk bolt upright, this day bow as meek as wheat:
how can I be sure I shall not always fear to face fierce heat,
to face the sun, not watch my shadow lagging back behind,
     and feel complete?

From strips of many metals am I made. I grow beneath the sun
unevenly. I cannot cry lest the least tear should cool down one
soft element and strain the others. I am bland, bend to become

the thermostat which keeps my spirit burning low. One day I shall
perhaps be tried by a more humble, human fire which, blending all
my elements in one alloy, will let me stand upright, ready to fall.

Trevor Reeves

they're keeping tabs

every time i smile a hole
appears in the card in the file
at the computer bank
i'm plugged into –
they're keeping tabs,
even as i run scared
and haunting, another hole appears
which i'm not expected to dodge
as they bug my stumbles
aware of their hollow echo
when i pause,
tie my shoelace –
threading the holes
carefully – holes
in my teeth, shivering
as i labour, bent,
up george street to the bank
to have another hole punched:
i'm drawing out all my money
and i'm going to stand for election
and have a punch-up with the government –
they're keeping tabs,
as i stand in a hole in queen's gardens
preaching to the people who pass
unaware a pattern of holes
accompanied by tapes whirring
wormlike in my inner ear
is impressing itself into the card
at the computer bank –
they're keeping tabs:
my lawnmower, wife,
electronic magnolia cultivator –

my stamp collecting machine,
my poems,
are being loaded by robots
into their time lorry
at my house.
masses of switches are stirring in alaska –
far distant stars, out of sight, are spinning
signals to each other –
they're keeping tabs,
but my tirade in queen's gardens
goes on
while machinery burns
hollowness in my cranium
brain like blue vein cheese
berating punch-drunk pedestrians
screaming of my fateful fateful
fate
and my death
as i die –
but they're keeping tabs;
yes, another hole
and the card is a picture frame
its innards in tatters;
an arm has transferred this card
that my soul has sieved through
to a file-machine marked D
and the time lorry has arrived
in queen's gardens
and a robot emerges to push
my corpse into the hole
along with my stamp collecting machine,
my electronic magnolia cultivator,
lawnmower, wife,
and all my poems, including this
one:
they're keeping tabs,
and they've levelled dirt
over the hole and pedestrians are

mincing their sticky soft stiletto heels
over my sky
and packing my flesh and possessions
into a lightless holy bundle.
you may just hear D-file machine
humming softly over my card
at the computer bank;
i'm dead,
yes
i'm dead,
but they're keeping tabs –
they're keeping tabs

Mary Cresswell

Metastasis

Tiny and trapped – the littlest name
a bit of a buzz, a wing of flame

melts amber back into waves
unleashing ten thousand years:

dragons and fire flies, damsels and may
flies spring from resin to molten seas

in their turn, no longer pinned down
but going where wide fast rivers

flurries, freshets, fly, leap, sing
down the sides of all the world

to swamps to standing water
where the minutes start again.

Simon Williamson

Japan 2030

The robot writes
such wonderful poetry
it may win the Nobel Prize

Tony Beyer

Kron

kron left his hands and oesophagus
to complete their supper
while he ushered me through
to the yellow inducement room

his diction was so precise
that he had no need of gestures
and i soon began to regret
the distorts on my laughter tape

then the vibrations started again
and the walls pouched and sagged
and slid across the floor in ropes
of living yellow between our feet

friim he shouted can you hear me
and i looked up from what seemed
miles away at the alloy plates
on my console flickering

kron raised a thin blunt arm
and his robots hissed away
on their sleek baffles leaving
the brief-cassette inside me

he told me again that the task
would commence at earthrise
and that my reactor must be switched
to reserve in the meantime

before i was dismissed kron's hands
and the vulgar little thread
of pipe he was so coy about
came fluttering back to him

i thought once more how frail
my master's components were
his seamless casing and the bright
unjointed tubes it protected

as i trundled down the ramp
to the android garage i wondered
for the ten thousandth time
what power had assembled him

only later when i replaced
a damaged bypass coil did i
remember the vital questions
i had intended to ask

Louis Johnson

Love Among the Daleks

At first it does not compute; but later
a current skips a beat and a new ballgame
emerges. (Or consider that pride can take a fall
out of cold reason.) Told, perhaps, that love
is what ennobles and fires the human, hardens
resolve, makes worlds & wheels cohere to purpose,
imagine the novice Dalek, set to excel
and master the universe, who first decides to outdo
the suburban Casanova at mating games
and makes his first call.
      But its object – a petrol pump –
is utterly heterosexual and is also involved
injecting its juices of life in the eager aperture
of a fast, pulsating car. 'Git lorst…,' it rasps,
guilty at side-of-the-mouth: and before you can say
'Exterminate' – the Dalek, who was not computed to fail –
blows his stack and electrodes and is wheeled off
to the parts department.
      Though Dalek authority
rails, raves, propagandises, nothing diverts their young
from the new goal – a notch or two in the studbook
of the propagation of the species. And so the universe
gets saved again – almost in spite of itself and
its cloudy gods – and this time without Dr Who,
absent on leave for identity ratification.
Which gives us a breathing space. At the last report,
a pack of the Dalek mods in leather trim
blazoned in white letters, 'The Onion Bunch',
and fully absorbed in the heat of their salad days,
bristled up Main Street pursuing the town bike.

26.8.78

Seán McMahon

planet one

8th dimension post max headroom
tv shows metagalactic adventure

buckaroo bonzai cosmic clip zip
code citizens dyslexic newscast

digital media strip evangelists
ultramodern qvc cable salvation

minitel message telematic phone
company sex receiver autogenous

dial tone connexion cue hang-up
hologrammatic spectrum emission

subliminal comicscope disney id
instincts copycat advertisement

billboard desires cartoon clock
work eleventh hour psychoactive

crisis cults cryptic hoopla jam
freeway spying cypher pseudonym

panic bodies cystoxic pharmakon
catastrophes agent.o alienation

panoptic pulsars infractal gaze
surveillance sectors simulacrum

Janis Freegard

Beside the Laughing Kitchen

I've been past the unbelievable planet:
Slabs of nostalgia, the soft skin of memory

Disruptive days, now swiftly approaching
For a stolen second I was myself again

I've been squeezing out the careful old songs
Eyes up looking, lights down dancing

Irregular obsession, beside the laughing kitchen
Tell me again, in empty eyelid sleep

Just how you got here: overgrown and delicate
Anxiously correct in curtained ballrooms

Thomas Mitchell

Rituals

My cryogenic sleep begins today,
so I remake this bed, one last time,
taking care to do it well,
without knowing when I'll need it next.
The woollen blanket, feather pillows and pressed cotton sheets,
objects the radio says are now so hard to get hold of,
spread over the mattress, their corrugations
more inevitable than the recovery the doctors promise,
a full cure for the cancer inside me, all activity postponed
until then, my body flattened in rest
like the shaking out of a soft, old quilt.

Alan Brunton

Vis Imaginativa

(Bringing her in):
there is not one day I do not
dream of you
Miss XO,
your frozen genes about to land on Earth
from your sprightly planet –
Therefore, let me ride with you
through generations of animals
preceded by generations
of the same animal
and speak in their rosettas jauntily
So, *let op!*
let me ride
until everything from A to burning Zee
is written with commas
like the commentary of blind masseuses
at an upstart's execution
commencing with the base pair La La
or a + b,
vivace:
the boomer whale's supersonic song!
Yes, we shall vamoose
as the desert moves in
sowing silicas in myrtle trees
and nothing will survive that is not the right size
and life itself
reverts to water and carbon and incongruity
Miss XO,
let me accompany you
to your star if necessary
where no wells are dry
and everything is Yippee and hot and On The Go

and each word has more rooms
than a box office attraction's chateau
Miss XO
let's go that far,
once around the showroom in your car
Miss XO,
I'm 'Here…'

Harvey McQueen

After The Disaster

After the disaster cats mutated
& became the largest mammal left alive –
dominant.

Cirques have cut deeper
into the Matterhorn
(decimals weren't reinvented)
when their archaeologists stumbled
upon human skeletons
ochre-brown with age.

On display in an art cavern
strung together
with common titanium wire
they create a commotion.

The elevated chief wizard deliberates her theosophers –
issues a viewpoint
       Carbane dating establishes grate antiquity
       Credence to archeforms of gyants
       These things – an evolutionary cul-de-sack
              additional proof of Nurture's
                 Distinguished Wisdom
       Greatly too gygantic
       Irrelevant clavicles
       Tayl (obviously grystle) long stretch from brayn
       Competition most likely cause of destruction.

She announces
        Dividend –
        For exceptional tripled production –
        Day off for druid & artisan multitude
        To contemplate the exhibition
        & participate
                in being humble.

Jenny Argante

Space Age Lover

Let me be your space age lover,
teleporting to your bed.
In a psychical intrusion
let me reach inside your head.
I will lock in circuits with you
for a trans-galactic surge
in molecular abandon
as our atoms blend and merge.

In the magic fourth dimension
we will time-warp up to Mars
popping love pills by the dozen
as we sport among the stars.
We will conquer time and motion
in the saucer-bowl of space
and my kisses burn like lasers
as I rush you back to base.

I will lunar-bug it to you
from the mountains of the moon.
I will set your robots dancing
to an electronic croon.
I will bleep you down a sunbeam,
make the rainbow's bend unfurl,
and we'll tumble down the aeons
in a planetary whirl.

As our eyes transmit a message
in a rocket-orbit blink,
we'll unzip spacesuits together
and we'll transformation-link
in a mind-exploding fusion,
love-entangled on your bed:
let me be your space-age lover,
let me reach inside your head.

Chris Else

Hypnogogia

Look, this is a stupid situation.
I can't sleep. She can't sleep.
Well, I could sleep maybe, if she'd let me.
Problem is I snore. Well, she says I snore.
And I believe her. I mostly believe her.
Sometimes I hear myself snoring.
Except that if I can hear myself,
I can't be asleep. And if I'm awake,
I'm not entirely sure that it can be counted
as snoring. Can it? Anyway,
the situation is this. I start to drift off,
I start to float through that penumbral world
where you see things that don't exist
and I start to snore. That wakes her up.
So then she wakes me up. 'Stop snoring!'
she says. And then we lie there.
She's too tense to go to sleep because
she's waiting for me to start snoring again
and I can't go to sleep because I'm worried
that I'll snore and wake her up.
Even though she isn't asleep. But
she wants to be. Of course. We both do.
And the trouble is that if only she'd let me
snore for a while, for maybe no more
than a minute or two I'd pass right through
that semi-conscious state and drift into
the nothing on the other side. And I'd stop.
But I can't tell her that. Snoring
is one of those things that nobody
has a right to. You're allowed it if
you can get away with it but not otherwise.

I mean, if we were both asleep and I was snoring,
who would care? Although, maybe it wouldn't
be snoring if nobody could hear it. It's like
that tree in the forest that doesn't make
a sound. At least, it doesn't make a sound
in my half-asleep world. Not that there are
many trees there. It's mostly buildings.
Mostly I feel like I'm floating along, as if
I'm driving in a convertible with the top back
and the sky is soft blue-grey, like down,
and I'm looking up at the buildings drifting past
on either side. There are houses sometimes, brick
with red tiled roofs and little wooden window boxes
full of flowers. And there are office blocks
and churches. And I only get a glimpse of them.
I'm only there for a second. Because if I say
to myself, 'Ah, yes, I'm here again,' it wakes me up and if
I don't, I go to sleep and it all disappears. Although,
maybe it doesn't. Maybe it's me that disappears.
Maybe there's a real world there on the other side of being
awake, a world full of life and energy and goings-on,
a world in which I don't exist. Although I glimpse it
sometimes through that hole in time and space
before the dark comes down and I wonder if,
for a moment, in that moment, I am there
and visible to the people in those streets,
an apparition hovering for a second
on the cusp of life. Do I frighten them?
Or do they know I'm just a phantom
passing through?

James Norcliffe

the ascent

he had expected deodorant
but what oozed through
the rotating slippery ball
was not what he'd expected

the bathroom filled with
a radiance he was forced
to filter through his eyelids
so that it throbbed with

his heart and glowed so
red with his pulsing blood
he was suffused with it
and then when it whispered

in a soft lubricating voice
scented with eucalyptus
he was suborned and born
anew he was climbing

the steaming stairs of
himself higher ever
higher to the warmer
mists where the mirror

beckoned where what
seemed to be love waited
with partly opened lips

where he disappeared

Fleur Adcock

from **Gas**

2

It was gas, we think.
Insects and reptiles survived it
and most of the birds;
also the larger mammals – grown
cattle, a few sheep,
horses, the landlord's Alsatian
(I shall miss the cats)
and, in this village, about a
fifth of the people.
It culled scientifically
within a fixed range,
sparing the insignificant
and the chosen strong.
It let us sleep for fourteen hours
and wake, not caring
whether we woke or not, in a
soft antiseptic
silence. There was a faint odour
of furniture-wax.
We know now, of course, more or less
what happened, but then
it was rather puzzling: to wake
from a thick dark sleep
lying on the carpeted floor
in the saloon bar
of the Coach and Horses; to sense
others lying near,
very still; and nearest to me
this new second self.

5

It is the sixth day
now, and nothing much has happened.
Those of us who are
double (all the living ones) go
about our business.
The two Mrs Hudsons bake bread
in the pub kitchen
and contrive meals from what is left –
few shops are open.
The two Patricks serve in the bar
(Bill Hudson is dead).
I and my new sister stay here –
it seems easiest –
and help with the housework; sometimes
we go for walks, or
play darts or chess, finding ourselves
not as evenly
matched as we might have expected:
our capacity
is equal, but our moods vary.
These things occupy
the nights – none of us needs sleep now.
Only the dead sleep
laid out in all the beds upstairs.
They do not decay,
(some effect of the gas) and this
seemed a practical
and not irreverent means of
dealing with them. My
dead friend from London
and a housemaid from the hotel
lie in the bedroom
where we two go to change our clothes.
This evening when we
had done our hair before dinner
we combed and arranged
theirs too.

6

Saturday night in the bar; eight couples
fill it well enough: twin schoolteachers, two
of the young man from the garage, four girls
from the shop next door, some lads from the farms.
These woodenly try to chat up the girls,
but without heart. There is no sex now, when
each has his undeniable partner,
and no eyes or hands for any other.
Division, not union, is the way we
must reproduce now. Nor can one think with
desire or even curiosity
of one's identical other. How lust
for what is utterly familiar?
How place an auto-erotic hand on
a thigh which matches one's own? So we chat
about local events: the twin calves born,
it seems, on every farm; the corpse
in a well, and the water quite unspoiled;
the Post Office reopened, but with no
telephone links to places further than
the next town – just as there are no programmes
on television or radio, and
the single newspaper that we have seen
(a local one) contained only poems.
No one cares much for communication
outside this circle. I am forgetting
my work in London, my old concerns (we
laugh about the unpaid rent, the office
unmanned, the overdue library books).
They did a good job, whoever they were.

8

This is becoming ridiculous:
the gas visits us regularly,
dealing out death or duplication.
I am eight people now – and four dead
(these propped up against the trees in the
gardens, by the gravel walk). We eight
have inherited the pub, and shall,
if we continue to display our
qualities of durability,
inherit the village, God help us.
I see my image everywhere –
feeding the hens, hoeing the spinach,
peeling the potatoes, devising
a clever dish with cabbage and eggs.
I am responsible with and for
all. If B (we go by letters now)
forgets to light the fire, I likewise
have forgotten. If C breaks a cup
we all broke it. I am eight people,
a kind of octopus or spider,
and I cannot say it pleases me.
Sitting through our long sleepless nights, we
no longer play chess or poker (eight
identical hands, in which only
the cards are different). Now, instead,
we plan our death. Not quite suicide,
but a childish game: when the gas comes
(we can predict the time within a
margin of two days) we shall take care
to be in dangerous places. I can
see us all, wading in the river
for hours, taking long baths, finding
ladders and climbing to paint windows
on the third storey. It will be fun –
something, at last, to entertain us.

9

Winter. The village is silent –
no lights in the windows, and
a corpse in every snowdrift.
The electricity failed
months ago. We have chopped down half
the orchard for firewood,
and live on the apples we picked
in autumn. (That was a fine
harvest-day: three of us fell down
from high trees when the gas came.)
One way and another, in fact,
we are reduced now to two –
it can never be one alone,
for the survivor always
wakes with a twin.
                    We have great hopes
of the snow. At this moment
she is standing outside in it
like Socrates. We work shifts,
two hours each. But this evening
when gas-time will be closer
we are going to take blankets
and make up beds in the snow –
as if we were still capable
of sleep. And indeed, it may
come to us there: our only sleep.

10

Come, gentle gas

I lie and look at the night.
The stars look normal enough –
it has nothing to do with them –
and no new satellite
or comet has shown itself.
There is nothing up there to blame.

Come from wherever

She is quiet by my side.
I cannot see her breath
in the frost-purified air.
I would say she had died
if so natural a death
were possible now, here.

Come with what death there is

You have killed almost a score
of the bodies you made
from my basic design.
I offer you two more.
Let the mould be destroyed:
it is no longer mine.

Come, then, secret scented double-dealing gas.
We are cold: come and warm us.
We are tired: come and lull us.
Complete us.
Come. Please.

ET

Vivienne Plumb

Signs of Activity

Prepare for contact. *The Alien Abduction Survival Guide* advises us to watch for elliptical, fuselage, or ovoid-shaped craft. Or watch out for little people. They could be pale blue in colour, gold, bright purple or even red with yellow wig-like hair.

Betty W. described being abducted while under regression therapy. Millions of people have had encounters with alien beings without realising it. Have you ever woken with a start? Have you any strange scars in the roof of your mouth or behind your ears?

One night we thought we heard a UFO take off outside. Larry was in bed. So I told Larry to get up quick and take a good look. But he wouldn't. I said to Larry, *it's a sad day when we miss meeting the aliens because you couldn't be bothered getting out of bed.*

Michael Morrissey

UFOs in Autumn

Among fixed stars   one moving
rather than shooting   it appears to knock
against   other pinboard lights

a clever Japanese game   that two
can play   I push/you pull
& the Galaxy lights up

but Herr Einstein is frowning
no celestial dice for Albert
no miracles of rare device

it's the hidden technology of sunsets
the UFO we've been
sciencefictionally prepared for

how cheekily you dance
— as though clipped from an angel's wing
you were swimming in heaven's light

space invader you win the world
tonight   I grant you sovereignty
over space ship earth

no weightier than a shadow
you'll land at my feet
the beautiful pilot speaking the language

of my choice
a mind to mind affair
favourably affecting my IQ

but you fly on overhead
like a brave thought-balloon
cut loose from the comic book brain

of its maker

Andrew Fagan

A Spaceship Has Landed Near Nuhaka

A magnificent cheese
Inviting field mice to nibble
In unsuspecting ignorance
A new breed roam the land
New faces for afternoon tea,
Best biscuits, best crockery
A chance to wear that dress from Gisborne
Tea stained pamphlets on the toilet floor
Bewilderment
A space ship has landed near Nuhaka

Dana Bryce

Dreams of Alien Love

I hope when I reach out
this time, I will feel a different skin.
Not coarse like the dark boy of yesterday or
pale and blue-veined fragile of the girl of last week,
but truly different.
A slow oozing of foreign musk,
a slickness from an organ with no terrestrial name,
a feeling of warmth that might kill a human lover.
Oh, I will take my chance with you,
for a new touch, a new taste of skin
acid, or sweet like primrose. To touch you
behind the third knee, under something I cannot see,
to clasp you as you die.
(I pray for beauty, but even if you
be like Caliban, I will love you)
To show you a human body,
to teach you to retract your claws like a loving cat;
I wait for you to whisper words with no meaning,
with a tongue I cannot hear.

Tracie McBride

Contact

Once,
the idea of sex with aliens
might have appealed.

But,
having encountered
your loathsome race,
I am cured
of my deviancy.

You,
with your putrid salty stench,
your pore-pitted skin
oozing at the mere
mention of heat.

You,
with appendages
upon appendages
dangling from your
spongy carapace.

You,
with your tiny globular eyes,
your chaotic, misfiring brain,
and that blind pink parasite
squirming inside your mouth.

It's enough to turn
all three
of my stomachs.

Cliff Fell

In Truth or Consequences

Police car sirens howling in the night –
I came down from the mountains to the big river
past rundown shacks and alleyways
to the Riverbed Hot Springs Trailer Camp

and into UFO country –
on a terrace of moonlit pools
Old Spirit Walking pulled me aside
claiming he was a spook in 'Nam
with high security clearance – Ultra 5…

      Yuh goin' to Roswell? –

Needless to say he knew it all
Everything seeded by the Roswell machine –

      fibre optics silicon chip the Pezio effect

his fingertips gripped tighter on my arm
eyelids blinking as in a trance

            It's all at Wright Paterson, man, Ohio
            There's a clean area
            A hangar where everything ET goes

            Yuh seen them Piggly Wiggly trucks on I-40?
            Delivering stuff to 51
            Onto 99 at Loughlin, or King City, man
            And the dirt road from there –

            That's all I can say
            But you're from down Australia way, man – so you should know
            There's an Area 42 there

the moon made a halo of his head
the river shone like a long white bone
and Old Turtle Mountain showed in silhouette
– where Billy the Kid holed up for days
out on the edge of Dead Man's Journey –

a coyote yipped in the cold river wind
a muskrat went splashing through the reeds
his wife like a shadow appeared at his side
        to lead him slowly away

Nelson Wattie

The Art of Translation

In a language spoken
On another planet
Interweaving
A distant double star
Far, far from here,
A beautiful poet wrote
Of a hairy, determined flower
Yearning out
From a deep crevasse
Towards the purple light.

Its desperation was overcome,
At least in part,
By its spirit,
And differently by the cold
Sand and burning
Light that tortured
Its twisted body.

When I came to translate
The beautiful poet's distant verse
Into my local Chinese,
So grounded on continent and village,
I sang, stilly and finely,
Of a wounded ox
Pulling my overfilled cart
Slowly, painfully,
Through a clogging
Mud-baked field
To save the children I love
From pitiful starvation.

Phil Kawana

This machine kills aliens

I kill aliens
from the safety of my
capsule

They explode in bloodless
supernova

While I sit in safety
at my little console

Self-contained
Self-confident
and self-appointed

Guardian of The Sky
Lion of Terra
The Silent Death

History's first
Ergonomic Samurai

From humble beginnings
I have arisen
Like a fiery phoenix…
From mild-mannered clerk
to the Upholder of Truth
Justice
and longer coffee breaks

(all to enable more
killing of aliens, of course)

But beware,
for the aliens are coming
they may be among us
RIGHT NOW!
Posing as one of us
Trying to be part of the group

I will not shirk my sworn duty
I shall not rest (any more than is necessary)

For I kill aliens

Remember,
Watch the skies…

Michael Morrissey

Are the Andromedans Like Us

or are they ghostly as nebulae
at the bottom of a banana milkshake
do the Andromedans go to church on sunday
mow their lawns on saturday
go on crash diets
do the Andromedans
open accounts on cosmic credit cards
which their inadequate Andromedan assets
cannot possibly cope with
are the Andromedans
strange undulations through methane seas
do Andromedan poets stare up at the sky
and wonder
if we are a thought in the mind
of the Milky Way
do the Andromedans copulate for thousands of years
in order to produce intergalactic twins
who cannot utter a single word
do millions of Andromedans have to hold hands
or other organs
to make a single Andromedan child
are the Andromedans closer to God
are they firsting the cosmic race
to make their own universe
I don't know
God doesn't know
and neither do the Andromedans

Mark Pirie

Dan and His Amazing Cat

Hi, I don't really know how to go about this
but I have an idea for a poem
that you might like to consider.

It is called 'Dan and his Amazing Cat'
and is set in the future on a
desert, wasteland planet,

where humans live with
and among aliens. The story
is about a boy called Dan

who lives with his grandfather in an iron mining
establishment where they have to
work long back-breaking hours to make a

living. With the help of his cat
they set to work in building a rocket ship
from scrap materials found at the junkyard,

James and his cat complete the rocket –
ship and get laughed at by all the other aliens
and people at the place they live in.

James has to overcome superior robots and
cheating aliens in order to find his way out.
And at the same time feed his cat.

As I'm not an SF writer, someone else can write it
for me perhaps – I'm quite a good illustrator though
and would love to illustrate the poem with detailed pictures.

James Dignan

Great Minds

Car. Open countryside.
Open road stretching out to meet the horizon.
To the left, a slumbering sea; to the right, a barren hillside.
Soft white ceiling of cloud.
Gravel flying as the car barrels down to the beach below.

Space. Inky night.
Hard brilliance of stars stretching out to meet forever.
To the left, a sheer wall of ocean; to the right, an empty infinity.
Soft blue curve of atmosphere.
Metal heating as the ship tumbles down to the globe below.

The car comes to a halt.
Gulls stand, or pick their way among the rocks.
The air is calm and clear.
The driver gets out of the car, stretches, smiles,
And breathes the clean salt air.

Not far away,
        Across the water,
                Another holidaymaker
                        Enjoys a similar view.

Cath Randle

The Purple fantastic, feels like elastic, spangled and plastic ray gun

The aliens left Helen a present
They came in the dead of night
She wore her curlers and they had green twirlers
So they gave each other a fright
The aliens left Helen a present
Formed in the fires of the sun
It was a purple fantastic, feels like elastic, spangled and plastic ray gun.

Helen had no rifle experience
She wanted to know how it feels
She closed her eyes tight as she looked through the sights
And shot off her car's front wheels
Success left Helen excited
She saw why aliens have fun
With a purple fantastic, feels like elastic, spangled and plastic ray gun.

No one believed Helen's story
Of alien ships on her roof
Three high schools expired when she took aim and fired
And scientists suddenly had proof
Helen became very possessive
Hers was the only one
A purple fantastic, feels like elastic, spangled and plastic ray gun.

She never left her gun unattended
She slept with the gun in her bed
One night all of a sudden, she pushed the wrong button
And woke up in the morning. DEAD
The moral is…
Never let spaced out technology
Take over your films or your life
Even if it's a purple fantastic, feels like elastic, spangled and
   plastic ray gun.

Jane Matheson

An Alien's Notes on first seeing a prunus-plum tree

This is a device for recycling air
…so intelligently functional in its design
yet aesthetically pleasing in its line.
These delicate rose-petalled flowers…
so soft to stroke, you can do it for hours!
It is wondrous too
that in the heat of the summer sun,
these flowers become
marble-sized ruby-red rounds
of delectable fruit-flesh.

Humans call it a prunus-plum tree
I would very much like
to take it back with me.

Harvey McQueen

Return

Great advance for a Gill. These cumbersome
uniforms work. Exhilaration mingles with
apprehension as Findolphin and I exchange
thumbs up. The first time our species has
left the water. The star-sparkles are brighter
and appear closer here above the safety zone.
Cautiously, slowly we flip to the wall of
earth-weed that merges into the sand.
Difficult to cut, stems are tougher than
we anticipated. The gigantic growth
overhead is beyond our reach. Voice
tells us time to start our return.

                                 Legend
has it that our ancestors once lived on
this shore & bred our gills to farm the sea.
Radical theologians reject this. Our elegance
has no need for such superstition, outmoded
like original sin. But it remains, a satisfying myth.

What's this? A strange menacing creature
– looks like a seal with legs like a lobster
two fewer, baring teeth as it circles us.
We fumble backwards towards the foam.
Suddenly it lunges. Its claws pierce
Findolphin's suit. The life-support
water flows out. I hesitate. Should I assist
him or get our specimens back. I seek advice.
Assist him they say. But a glance shows me
he is beyond aid the animal tearing at his
apparel & – horror – his flesh. His look of
anguish I'll never forget. Obviously a type

of land-shark. As more of the monster's
kind burst out of the undergrowth I retreat.
I do not think we will ever survive in that
environment. My report is not well-received.
They build an obelisk on the outer side of
the reef to us but they make it clear I should
have died a martyr. For my cowardice they
condemn me. I now extract sea-snake venom.

Owen Marshall

Awakening

Life is but a dream the old song tells us
so what will be its joyous awakening.
What odd, alternative society will we
return to and share a fading recollection
of this time. What purple multi-mooned

sky, what novel vapours, what monstrous
company in which we are perfectly at home
flourishing a webbed membrane to subdue
incredulity as we recount a fantasy of
caged animals and AIDS, Gotham city arcades

silicon celebrities, children burned with
napalm bombs, and gleaming whales sunk in
poisonous seas. Our fellow creatures will
work their orifices and antennae to signal
joy that no such place could possibly exist.

Peter Bland

An Old Man and Science Fiction

The neighbours cut the world to fit their pockets.
Now his were empty. His tramcar talk,
of no direct concern, revolved
around the village of his birth. What
worth to them, whose lives ran straight
between the office and the garden gate,
the weekend roast and all-consuming bed?

His company refused, he turned to other worlds
outside the scope of heaven and hell,
where skin-tight blondes
wear fish-bowls on their heads
and copulate with Martians deep in space.
Packing up a life that no one wanted
he left and felt the old world shrink

beneath his feet. The neatly laid-out houses
disappeared. Children ceased
their taunting in the streets. No
welcoming areas awaited his return.
Death would be a burn-out. Lost in space
he'd float as a cloud-shine, there forever
adrift between raw gravity and grace.

When Worlds Collide

Katherine Liddy

Crab Nebula

They snap the blue, still-glamorous star,
the astronomy paparazzi, rapt: her corpse
ripe opportunity, her gaseous face
an enormous light clot leaking out
to stain the giant bath of space.

The telescope crowd absorbs her importance,
admires the electric silk of her filaments,
and traces with ravenous eyes the hoard
of jewel lights and colourful elements.
If these are her relics then what was her life?
The bystanders wonder, regret that they missed
the scene of quick change, the second she burst
into flash last millennium, the splinter of doubt
between her being whole and her non-being,
but this will do for now. The bloom of death
is something apart, remains consuming.

The spillage has all she had. Though crushed
or changed the basic arrangements exist.
The distant voyeurs warm their brains
at white-hot threads, forked-lightning arms
backed by a brilliant blue continuum
and, at dead centre, the neutron star,
her heart, the burning ball of pulsar
the size of some town, the mass of earth's sun
but brighter, of denser matter. It twists,
a souvenir of grandeur not quite gone,
a chandelier in a shipwreck, burning on.

Anna Jackson

Death Star

Outstare the stars. Infinite foretime and
Infinite aftertime: above your head
They close like giant wings, and you are dead.
— Nabakov, **Pale Fire**

The extinction of the dinosaurs
was just the last

of the mass extinctions
of the past:

five we know of, tens of millions
of years apart.

It could be a 'Death Star' orbits
with our sun,

every few billion years
pulling down

a storm of asteroids like the one
that killed the dinosaurs,

punctuating a history
of cataclysms

of extinction, ecosystems
collapsing in disarray.

The most recent mass extinction
began a few thousand years ago,

when people took in great numbers
to the sea,

colonised, farmed,
industrialised.

We are losing species at a hundred times
the natural rate, a thousand times,

and the rates of extinction
are increasing.

We have become
our own Death Star.

Stephen Oliver

Manned Mission to the Green Planet

Behind some night bush Rousseau green,
some dwelling in one place, some in another,
it had been agreed between us by courier
and hesitation to meet in the village centre
at midnight. The first figure to emerge
was to be greeted thus: *America comes to
interpret its humour:* the hurried reply;
community halls abound. Back, beyond our
allotted frequency, The General who had
not been posted gathered over another Power
Lunch. After the brief and the oiling of
rifles we set forth across the causeway
through the marble green of foothills,
into the grey of higher ground. The thought,
like a saffron scarf caught on a thorn
bush seemed even now on the closed terrain a
crusade of sorts – kept us ahead. Amply,
unnumbered rivers plashed into the battery
green of immeasurable hollows. So it was
that we became inseparable, spirit creatures
to the forest life, the journey boundless,
the orders which concerned the depot, unread.

Hilaire Kirkland

Three Poems

I

A thing fled from daylight:
          refuge
in the huge hollowness of night-among-stars.
A bead which spirals sparkling down the swinging string
          of memory, linking
the warm-wombed earth to her wan child the moon.
And far-off lights, flung through space
          (haphazard, heaped, dice on a dark cloth)
flare and gutter as candles in a
wind-washed black-boughed tree.
But none to see the pendant bead
          – binding a warm white throat, on a gold thread –
or remember the scent of pine in the rain.

II

Comet: insane spawn of a sick sun.
crimson clot of blood that scrawls
across burning skies.
Fine thin fire interwoven, patterned without reason,
knitting a weird net of copper wire
To trap some star.
The bone-white moon.
Polished skeleton, stark skull staring,
dead marble floating in the night,
lip-lapped by waves of black
breaking on white beaches,
washed by long silences that flow from space.

To whimper up channelled ways, and soundless,
ache in desert reaches
and cliff caves.
And on the moon an alien shadow flickers –
once – bright bead:
a blackened smudge upon a wall
or else a warmth-bewildered bee that crawls and licks
the honey-scented flower,
or a scorched moth in the hot night
whirring round an opalescent ball.
Bright eye winking eye everglowing –
earth's brittle gift to her white child
        lift and fall
pulsing thing come to this
high, pale timeless world.

III

Men say: 'The moon, there no God is
for no man is, to praise.
only emptiness, a cold fantastic pastoral.'
        I remember the brown bee
        on a giant, tousled, yellow flower –
        the cut grass, a garden singing with summer
        (flowers in the garden on earth in the summer)
        yet here there is none to see.
Who shall decide where God is?
Where night upon heavy night slumbers in channelled ways.
age after age piles high,
a sifted dust that
stifles the white plain in sleep.
long slow tides of silence creep
into oceans without ships, and lick the bone dry bays
and whisper on untrodden shores
        and ebb, and flow –
and who shall say
if this is God, or no?

Michael O'Leary

Hey man, Wow! [Jimi Hendrix]

*(from the cricket novel **Out of It**)*

Hey man, Wow! Like the white streak
Of power that provides the purple haze
Which is the universe propelling projectiles
Such as the Red Planet of Mars towards me
The centre of the star-spangled galaxy

There is a theory such as reverse energy
Matter which interpreted into reality
Means, if I flick this switch that's in
My hand in the opposite direction, Mars
Will go flyin', I mean flyin', back

Through the same galaxy of time and space
And over the boundary of infinity
Into eternity – far out, man!
Outside in the distance the wind cries
As the man who is as lost as a child

Throws his round red ball towards
My bat which I hold erect, yeah man!
The wind cries because this blood red ball
Pierces the skin of the air: the wind cries
With the awareness of its own existence

But the ball keeps coming and coming until it hits my
Bat mid-on, and I'm running and the wind is crying…

Robin Fry

Lift-off

'Oh we're ten years away from it yet,'
he said, his large eyes glowing.
There's a flame that burns inside him
like the gas jet that lifts an air balloon.
In the night I hear it hissing while he sleeps.
'I live to go to Mars,' he said.

Did I choose to be a widow
like Mrs Cook?
While the Captain met his death
in distant islands
she merely grew old.

Women like us
live in the base camps of such men.
Like scientists, they are another breed.

What if he takes our sons with him?
In ten years they will be grown men.

Outside their door at night
I listen
for that hiss.

Tim Jones

Touchdown

The engine ceased and silence fell.
We had made it. Nine months,
nine months in a metal womb
drinking recycled urine
eating recycled crap
watching our dosimeters glow.

I earned my place as captain. Sure,
there was the PR angle: Venus flies to Mars!
Great for the ratings, all that sort of thing.
But a dream born in girlhood
honed through years of preparation
had fitted me to take command.

'We're down,' I said, 'we're clear and down.'
Fifteen minutes later
they would be cheering the news in Houston
but for now we had the planet to ourselves.
I looked at my companions. Dazed, exhausted,
but a spring of joy flowed in every one.

A human was about to step on Mars. The moment
I had dreamt about had come. I crawled into the airlock.
I waited till it cycled. I stepped outside
and felt the Martian sun.
The cold air chilled me. The red light was eerie.
The great deed of my life was done.

Tim Jones

The First Artist on Mars

Well, the first *professional* artist.
There were scientists who, you know,
dabbled
but NASA sent us –
me and two photographers –
to build support for the program.

The best day?
That was in Marineris.
Those canyons are huge
each wall a planet
turned on its side.
I did a power of painting there.

You can see all my work
at the opening. *Do* come.
Hey, they wanted me to paint propaganda –
you know, 'our brave scientists at work' –
but I told them
you'll get nothing but the truth from me

I just paint what I see
and let others worry
what the public think.
Still, the agency can't be too displeased.
They're sponsoring my touring show.
That's coming up next spring.

Would I go back? Don't know.
It's a hell of a distance
and my muscles almost got flabby
in the low G. Took me ages

to recover – lots of gym and water time
when I should have been painting.

But Jupiter would be worth the trip!
Those are awesome landscapes
those moons, each one's so different.
Mars is OK – so old, so red,
so vertical. Quite a place
but limited, you know?

Puri Alvarez

Saturn's Rings

Where, out of the many rooms of time,
does this box of sound belong?
It contains the tides of infinity.

After meeting myself in the mirror of your eyes,
I remembered when I saw you last.
It must have been further than a light year away
and you whispered to me:
'Even from the edge of Saturn's rings
the answer to those questions that belong to Eternity,
the answer, I say, is love.'

Robert Sullivan

from **Star Waka**

iv 2140AD

Waka reaches for stars – mission control clears us for launch
and we are off to check the guidance system
personally. Some gods are Greek to us Polynesians,
who have lost touch with the Aryan mythology,
but we recognise ours and others – Ranginui and his cloak,
and those of us who have seen *Fantasia* know Diana
and the host of beautiful satyrs and fauns.

We are off to consult with the top boss,
to ask for sovereignty and how to get this
from policy into action back home.
Just then the rocket runs out of fuel –
we didn't have enough cash for a full tank –
so we drift into an orbit we cannot escape from
until a police escort vehicle tows us back

and fines us the equivalent of the fiscal envelope
signed a hundred and fifty years ago.

They confiscate the rocket ship, the only thing
all the iwi agreed to purchase with the last down payment.

46

it is feasible that we will enter

space
colonise planets call our spacecraft *waka*

perhaps name them after the first fleet
erect marae transport carvers renew stories
with celestial import

establish new forms of verse
free ourselves of the need for politics
and concentrate on beauty

like the release from gravity
orbit an image until it is absorbed
through the layers of skin

spin it
sniff and stroke the object
become poetic

oh to be in that generation
to write in freefall picking up the tools
our culture has given us

and to let them go again
knowing they won't hit anyone
just stay up there

no longer subject to peculiarities
of climate the political economies
of powers and powerless

a space waka
rocketing to another orb
singing waiata to the spheres

Chris Pigott

'We're thinking of going into space'

We're thinking of going into space.
John's tired of the smell of grass
and automobiles, and women
are bringing him down. He can not
see very clearly now,
in space it's of no matter:
they have comets and asteroids
and a million little satellites up there
but the ship will drive itself.
That's what John wants
to give up the wheel,
to watch the blackness or blueness
or any other stinking colour
drift on by. Me, I'm just
out of rope. I hear in space
there's all kinds of nail and wood
to be had. This is my plan:
a space hut, for John and me,
where we can get the rhythm of the place,
where we can sit back, and where
we can give up the fight, at last.

Mark Pirie

Liam Going

Dear all

Today I'm leaving
not just my workplace
but the Entire Planet.

My best wishes to everyone,
I've enjoyed my 20+ years here,
and especially the company
and friendship
of so many of you.

I don't know what the future holds,
but one avenue I'm exploring is
an on-line space supply shop:
it's listed on the Department's
Interplanetary Bulletin Board.

I'm also available on contract
(unless I get snapped up by big money aliens)
for writing, editing, robot photography,
photo-editing, layout, space design,
and alien sound recording and editing.

I'm logging off now,
but you can contact me at
Planet Maxus (on the Space Net)
or spacemail me: liam2go@maxus

Ngā mihi o te ngākau ki a koutou kātoa

Iain Britton

Departing Takaparawha

A woman squats.
She's not peeing
or grubbing for worms.

She hugs her coffee
and stares at clouds
at islands in the gulf.

A man
cut from wood
and heavily tattooed

sits astride a gate
his penis
pointing at the sun.

Another man
the colour of dirt
comes to us

strips off his old clothes
and stands sweating
upright in the light.

In his house masked people
leap down from walls
and sit on the floor. They talk

and chant genealogies.
On the roof
someone

tugs strings,
works eyes
and limbs.

The show goes on.
We traipse outside
visibly swallowing the day.

A child (as if hatching)
crawls from her dugout
in the ground

and takes off.
A man crinkled like silver foil
tells us she has this passion

for re-enactments
for re-entering the earth's atmosphere
when she's ready.

Bill Sewell

The Imaginary Voyage

fascinated from the start
what methods they devised
to make that crossing:

the wings of large birds
strapped to their arms
a flock of swans in harness
a great many glasses full of Dew
and the gigantic cannon:

no world to mirror theirs
but dust rocks & a crystal sky
(though in the crater Tycho
they found nuggets of gold) –

later they ventured further
plunging into the mists
of the morning star
searching in vain for water
in the canals of Mars –

with these civilized & mined
they watched the sun
pale into the Galaxy
and grew old in the gulf
before Alpha Centauri –

they have seen
no glittering cities
nor golden oceans

only winking beacons
that no longer
give a course to steer by
(Canopus has grown dim
Aldebaran has fallen far behind):

Along Eridanus we drifted
Al Nahr the River of Heaven
drinking as we went
'the sweet poison of the false infinite' –

others call it the Ashen Path:
how many blazing
or burnt out worlds
did we encounter there –

we sought enchanted isles
full of sweet fragrance & sound
but found not even the lotus
nor the deadly singing voices:

Argo and past Andromeda
avoiding the sea monster Cetus
each time we sent off the dove
it came back with nothing.

Rachel Bush

Voyagers

Guided by stars and changes in the sun,
travelling with hope and uncertainty,
voyagers carried water, food and songs.
They looked for cloud as a sign of land to
discover. They had come so far. Over
and over they heard paddles dip in waves
and chants that made their shoulders move beyond
the ache of their work. They knew wherever
they arrived they would have changed.

Inside their metal capsule, voyagers
move with weightless care. They have left the curve
of the world, the pattern of continents.
Still guided from earth they seek, calculate,
measure, compute, discover, travel far
and farther through black quiet space, the brilliance
of unknown stars. When they return they have
changed.

We too are voyagers and will be changed.
We do not know where we will discover
our future, but know we must start with guides
we trust and then must travel beyond them.
We too can move with hope through unknown seas
towards far stars.

Stephen Oliver

Letter to an Astronomer

Starry amorist, starward gone,
– Francis Thompson

Make no mistake – we arrived here first, by pathways
mostly forgotten, hinted at maybe, in the clinging moss on
gutter and drain, by ruined foundations, under destroyed
civilizations. Look no more, we are the visitors we
seek come via starburst and interstellar dust, riding the cold
chariots of comets, destined to make the biggest splash: –
hominid, Neanderthal, homo-sapien sought to track back
to what 'Courtyard of the Gods', multiple or singular,
in search of the primal spark, can hardly be guessed at.
Our breath might be read within the banded spectrum
of your inquiry that magnifies the sky's falling domino;
by wingbeat of light fleeing across the great glass lens.

Looking down through the whirligig
                                   of immeasurable galaxies

will lead back again to the filmic awe over the retina as
you seek to locate by the interstices of deep space an echo
in nothingness. Granaries of knowledge (gravity's burden)
we laid down in ancient geologies; when we rested,
cities rose, when we walked, cities fell. Make no mistake
there'll be neither alien ship nor coded message exchanged,
merely (coming in under radar) signs of our passing
in time, most fluid of inventions – condemned forever to
rush forward, condemned forever to rush backward.
The orchard is rotten, the field beyond, cloaked in the
dandelion or wildflower waits for the plough or the sword.

Memory's digital code recounts something discarded,
as though God looked away for an instant after creation
and like uncertain visitors we fled from his hand as we fell.

January 14, 2000

The Final Frontier

Helen Rickerby

TABLOID HEADLINES

DOG GROWS MAN'S HANDS

MAN GROWS DOG'S HEAD

NUDE ARTISTS PAINT CLOTHED MODEL

PIGEON ROBS BANK

WOMAN WALKS ON WATER: 'NO I'M NOT THE
MESSIAH, I'M JUST VERY CLEVER'

3 MONTH OLD STANDS TRIAL ON MURDER CHARGE

HOUSE RUNS AWAY FROM HOME: 'IT WAS THERE
WHEN I LEFT FOR WORK'

SPORT MAD MAN'S HEAD BECOMES A RUGBY BALL

'ELVIS WAS MY MOTHER'

TIGER CUB GETS TOP MARK IN HISTORY EXAM

'THAT'S MR CYCLOPS TO YOU'

WOMAN MARRIES ALIEN EMPEROR: 'I ALWAYS WAS
AMBITIOUS'

MAN'S HEAD EXPLODES WHILE SHAVING

ALIEN EMPRESS POISONS NEW BRIDEGROOM,
BECOMES SOLE RULER OF 10 GALAXIES: 'I TOLD
YOU I WAS AMBITIOUS'

Sue Wootton

the verdigris critic

Suddenly tired
of the complicated interlacing of words in lyrical trim
she goes outside
and shouts very loudly
into the night.

The stars tremble
infinitesimally
then regroup.

In a distant time
on a distant planet
a literary critic with a greenish tinge
cups a tentacle to a blobular ear

hears UCK! UCK! UCK! UCK! UCK!
reverberate gently in the heavens.

Ah, sighs the verdigris critic.
Truly, poetry
is universal.

Richard von Sturmer

from **Mill Pond Poems**

III

Autumn leaves overlap
on the surface of the pond.
Minnows gather
beneath an empty boat.
Their world is
apparently seamless
while I am like that astronaut
in Tarkovsky's film
who returns to his father's house
and to the stillness
of a sleeping lake.

A momentary lapse
of concentration
(the slightest breeze will do)
and he knows that he will lose
the vine-covered pillars
the cracked steps
the golden light.

He knows that he will find himself
back in the depths of space.

Brian Turner

Earth Star

Before we commence, consider a proposition
we must ask, and examine, a question;
in this case a big question like, for instance,
What is the Universe?

To begin, then,
Why is it as it is?
Was there a Bang, rather biggish,
and is there, or was there, a Bumper?

Is, or was there a Whumper
become a Whimper? And will there be
a Mend before the End
or is it all without…? Was there a

beginning? What were conditions like:
think of the power of coincidence, of
'fine-tuning' states, circumstances,
of the mercurial skill in knowing

when and what and how to choose
'the' moment. And was there, is there
cognizance in cooperation? Is there God,
and whose God? Good God, are there

many 'worlds', and many Gods,
and is there one who is 'wholly good'?
(Things as they are are different
here than on another star, or are

they, and how are things with you
anyway, wherever you are?) Every
conceivable world exists. Nothing
ever exists. How are things

on Earth star? Which possibility
obtains, and why? is the question
you must put to the sky above
you. (Things as they are

are, far out there, are elsewhere,
better by far, better by … hah!)
Say, I will be true to you
but what caused you in the course

of time, over time? Are natural laws
the only real laws, and have they flaws,
and are you a once day wonder?
When your part of this world is good

why is it not as good more often,
and is it bad elsewhere
when it is good here? Good grief,
explain, select, be a randomeer.

But who is your real, true heir, here,
and who in time, or out, will care?
And are there others out there
beyond the stratosphere, quite near to here,

and will we, or others like us, one day soon
meet others, odder than us, playing
even odder, more peculiar tunes?
Surely not: surely, why not?

Gary Forrester

The Thirst That Can Never Be Slaked

In pursuit of Anna, Rusty circled the moon.
Spacesick in his module, his heartbeat
reached one hundred nine.

Into the burn of his lunar descent,
he calibrated landing zones
between the craters of his eyes.

After touchdown, the flight plan listed
rest, then extra-vehicular activity.
On impulse, Rusty raised the hatch,

shuffled down the ladder to the surface
of the moon. His left foot marked the dust
beside his lover. And so it was

he broadcast for the ages – earth words
for the still unborn: 'Woman,' Rusty spoke
into his air-tight helmet. 'Womankind.'

David Kārena-Holmes

Your Being

Your being is
a blazing star
that turns and burns
like Achernar,

like Fomalhaut
or Betelgeuse
in my darkling
universe.

A voyager
in time and space,
toward that light
I set my face.

John Dolan

In Which I Materialize, Horribly Maimed, in the Transporter Room of the *Enterprise*

I materialize in the *Enterprise* transporter room
with an old weathered pitchfork jammed in my back
and the bloody tines dripping onto the floor.
'Horror and compassion vie on their faces'
as they force themselves to take my arms and tenderly
bear me down to Sick Bay where Doctor McCoy's face
twists in rage: 'My GOD, Jim!
what kind of BARBARIANS would –'
then at a gesture from the captain, McCoy calms himself,
puts a painless pneumatic needle on my arm –
endorphins. Product of the finest twenty-fifth century
pharmaceutical research. No dirty cut heroin,
this is pleasure itself, pleasure incarnate, past argument.
They do what they can to ease
The little time I have left. They gather
round my antigravity couch as I wake,
try to smile. The same flinching awe
on all their faces as they stare at me. McCoy is crying.
Spock takes his place. The raised Vulcan eyebrow –
highest praise! He says evenly, 'It would appear…'
a pause – '… that you have …
suffered much.' Then, afraid to go too far,
he adds, '… For a human, at any rate.'
Ah, that last bit of bluff, no matter!
Spock is impressed! Spock! Then Kirk,
gesturing at the pitchfork, 'How did you … how could you …
live – walk – go on?'
I shrug. I am as good as the Mongols now!
To them I am Medieval!
I smile: '… In my day everyone … was like this.
It was … no big deal.' McCoy, appalled: 'NO BIG DEAL?'

Kirk motions him to silence, says quietly,
'You bear up well, Mister…?'
'Oh my name … doesn't matter. What year is this, Captain?'
And before he can answer I die.

Mark Pirie

The Rescue Mission

Captain's log: Planet Z, Dec 26ᵗʰ 2146

Spent all day
loading bodies
into the
newly-formed
crater.

Bits of
the new Galaxy
Tourism
Industry's
spaceship
were
embedded
in the remains.

We were
instructed
to remove
the fragments
at all cost,
for examination
back home;
money and
capital gain
were at stake
for entrepreneurs
and political gain
was definitely
at stake
for many
a ruler
on Earth.

I'd put
covers over
the worst
of them
faintly recalling
old film reconstructions of
Medieval Europe
with shallow
ditches along
roadsides.

Who'd ever
forget this;
not now,
at Xmas time.

'Are these
ones dismembered
or incinerated?'
Yuri asked.

'No, hold on, those go
in the other crater,'
I replied fearfully.

Edwards Jr
separating part of a leg
from planetary rock
swivelled round
complaining his
girlfriend'd
just txt'd him
holidaying
at Hanmer Springs:
*'Who'd be a thrill
seeker eh?'* she
piped in new
numeric code

scrambled through
space.

But Edwards Jr,
always the optimist,
txt'd her back
reminding her
that space travel
was never easy,

and Yuri now
trying to smile
with half a torso
piggy-backing
him said as
he jumped
into the crater, 'I
always knew
it'd
be like you Americans
say "one *hell* of
a joy-ride!"'

Tze Ming Mok

Lament of the imperfect copy of Ensign Harry Kim

Episode 5.18, Stardate 52586.3. As their bodies begin to degrade, the Voyager crew gradually discover that they are cloned copies of the original Voyager crew. The clone of Harry Kim is the first to die, in a cave while on reconnaissance.

Your quickening sunrise claws
through broken cornea
as we did, towards a
federal unity of design –
I cannot now remember
the motto's original wording,
something the opposite of
'WE are the Borg.
YOU will be assimilated'.
Imperfections rupturing my
cortex are blossoms
of doubt my original lacks.
How many copies
could there be, and if
we all heaved and leapt
as one to the ground, how many
forests would be heard
rising round the
other hemisphere?
If we stood end to end,
which moon would we reach,
and what walls would we see
from there? Feel for
all us Ensigns, each
slightly off like
Pound's calligraphy,
'gone and on the going',
every stroke a not-quite
Harry Kim; I am so damn

sick of him. As the eyes are
gone, and cavities
collapsing, let me slip off
behind our time's faint
surface glimmer, to where
I could have been
a Sulu, sitting with
presence and grace, as a
shogun's son on the open field
in Kurosawa's Ran, smiling
with fistfuls of unbroken
arrows. Or a Vulcan, a Klingon
or a liberated Borg. They have pride.
They mock us and are correct
in posture, uncontracted
in grammar, unshackled
in the main, like the
old man in Bladerunner, twittering
in Cantonese to his eyeballs
in the steaming vat, who
didn't have answers, he
just did eyes, or the
noodle-jockey who
wouldn't speak English
but watched Deckard
smooth splinters from chopsticks
in wait for the finish line,
yes, any of those garbled masses
run through in a
clamouring night by
some pale hero,
an army, an infinite
platoon of Eights –
sleepers to the bone,
never captured
in the *Daily Galactica* headline:
'Valeri shoots Captain, self',
watching our

adopted parents fall
as will falls – let me be
among them,
obstructive, closed and
let me not be called
'Harry'. To no longer
miss my unfleshed mama
or play Riker's white jazz on the clarinet
or have aced quantum mechanics
while never, ever getting laid, at all.
Already the twenty-fourth
century – so much time
wasted, and now none left
to eat even my own
wasted organs
with my bitterness,
to show contempt for
my last moment
on this foreign satellite.

Nic Hill

Somewhere Else

it is strange

to stand
on a world so small
that you can reach out with a glove
and touch the horizon

for the sun to be
a small light
among a multitude of others

for the face in the sky
to be a falling raging giant
with one red eye

to stand
on the shores of an ocean
that isn't made of water

home is years away
my mind
wasn't made for this
where else would I be
but here

Tim Jones

The stars, Natasha

Natasha, fundamentals are strong,
key indicators steady.
Leave your books, Natasha,
let your computer
draw patterns on its screen.

Walk with me through the heavens.
Along cold orbits
the spendthrift stars
squander their assets on light.
The World Bank

is unamused; the IMF
is noting down their names.
So take my hand
let's drift away
into the cosmic background.

Mike Webber

My Personal Universe

My universe
Where I make my verse
Is black and green
And mostly unseen
Galaxies and thoughts
A nebulous emerald
Stomach a supernova
Not easily filled
My cores have been drilled
My eyes saw through
Bore into
An almost blue
Black hole.

I will trust
Those that come to my crust
Save some of my worlds
That have the beauty of girl
Come and expand that language
To my green dark galaxy
My universe in spreading
Like golden honey
Across your tender buttery feminine toast
I move green suns and star clouds across
A cross word is never said
In my galaxy, my universe.

In my universe
I worship you
Under stars crossed with intensity
If I ever lose my propensity
For loving you

In my empty, void, dark, sparkling, magical
Universe of green and black
Send your rocket ships in
And bring me back.

Bill Sewell

Space & Time

a long time ago
in a galaxy far far away
are things that we know
and things that amaze —

lumbering space cruisers
with rows of winking lights
idle in orbit then glow
and vanish into the Milky Way
their crews ever youthful
in uniforms by Gucci:

the stars have closed together
no more endless waiting
for news of other worlds –

but where with all
this star-hopping it ends
who it was ignited
the big bang anyhow
and why the eternal
bickering & jostling
is a mystery as ever –

in the next millennium
on a planet in the system
of Sagittarius the legions
will march against a savage
tribe of forest-dwellers

the inhabitants of the ninth
planet of Altair enjoyed
a gravitational pull so weak
they floated in the air

in the constellation of Aquarius
the primeval soup has scarcely
begun to bubble:

between the stars
are whirlpools which
may suddenly suck you
into another galaxy
a long time ago
far & further away

and as you spin
you may be treated
to glimpses of worlds
before now & after –

what colours
and what confusion:
the journey to satisfy
your ever-probing eye.

Fleur Adcock was born in New Zealand and now lives in London. She received the Queen's Gold Medal for Poetry in 2006. Her poetry books include *Poems 1960-2000*. For more details and video see http://www.bloodaxebooks.com

Raewyn Alexander, from Hamilton, now an Aucklander, has a BIC from Unitec, and is an author of novels, stories, non-fiction and poetry. The Overload Poetry Festival, Melbourne, has invited her to read many times. Her latest poetry collection, *Museum of Lost Days*, is from the Earl of Seacliff Art Workshop, and Tiny Titles poetry books are sold around Auckland. See http://www.myspace.com/raewynalexander

Born in Spain and living permanently in New Zealand since 1995, **Puri Alvarez** has published work in both countries, mostly in anthologies and literary magazines. The extraordinary and the ordinary humanity, the supernatural as well as nature itself, are her sources of inspiration. She writes mostly poetry and short stories.

Jenny Argante is a Tauranga-based writer and professional editor, a member of the editorial team for *Bravado*, the literary arts magazine from the Bay of Plenty. She has been widely published in New Zealand, the UK and North America. Jenny most enjoys the challenges of poetry.

Tony Beyer writes and teaches in New Plymouth, Taranaki. His *Dream Boat: Selected Poems* was published by HeadworX in 2007. He edited the bi-annual collection *Poetry Aotearoa*, a selection of New Zealand poetry for Australian readers through Picaro Press, Sydney.

Peter Bland was born in Yorkshire, England, in 1934. He emigrated to New Zealand at age 20 where he met the 'Wellington Group' of poets. He has worked for many years as an actor, both in New Zealand and abroad, as well as a writer. He currently lives in England, where his *Selected Poems* appeared from Carcanet in 1998. His latest collection is *Mr Maui's Monologues* (Steele Roberts, 2008).

Iain Britton had his first collection of poems, *Hauled Head First into a Leviathan*, which was a Forward Poetry Prize nomination, published by Cinnamon Press (UK) in February 2008. Interactive Publications (Australia) will be publishing his second collection, *Liquefaction*, in 2009.

Alan Brunton (1946-2002) was a poet, scriptwriter, and performer, closely associated with the Red Mole theatre group. He was also the founding editor of *Freed* magazine in the late 1960s and the small press Bumper Books in the 1990s. A memorial page for Alan is at http://www.nzepc.auckland.ac.nz/authors/brunton/recollections.asp For further information, see http://www.bookcouncil.org.nz/writers/bruntonalan.html

Dana Bryce is a New Zealand poet.

Rachel Bush is a Nelson writer whose work has appeared in anthologies and in periodicals such as *Sport, Takahe, The Listener*, and the electronic journal *Turbine*. The most recent of her three books of poetry, *All Patients Report Here*, was published by Wai-te-ata Press in 2006.

Alistair Te Ariki Campbell was born in Rarotonga in 1925. He moved to New Zealand on the death of his parents in 1933. A prolific author, he has published four novels, a radio play, and 18 collections of poems, including most recently *Just Poetry* and *It's Love, Isn't It?: The Love Poems* (both from HeadworX). His many awards, including the Pacific Island Artists' Award and an Hon DLitt (from Victoria University of Wellington), culminated in an ONZM and a Prime Minister's Award for Literary Achievement in Poetry in 2005.

Meg Campbell (1937-2007), a well-known New Zealand poet, married the poet Alistair Te Ariki Campbell. They lived in Pukerua Bay for 47 years. Meg published six collections of poetry, beginning with *The Way Back*, which won the PEN Award for Best First Book of Poetry in 1982. Her final book, *Poems Adrift*, came out on 17 November 2007, a day after she died.

Gordon Challis was born in Wales in 1932. Emigrating to New Zealand in 1953, he studied at Victoria University of Wellington. He has worked as a journalist and social worker here and abroad. He now lives in Takaka, Golden Bay. His poetry books are *Building* (Caxton Press, 1963), *Other Side of the Brain* (Steele Roberts, 2003) and *Luck of the Bounce* (Steele Roberts, 2008).

Janet Charman's sixth collection, *cold snack* (AUP, 2007), won the 2008 Montana NZ Book Award for Poetry in 2008. Charman was Literary Fellow at the University of Auckland in 1997 and her recent work can be found online at: http://jacketmagazine.com/36/index.shtml Her website is http://www.nzepc. auckland.ac.nz/authors/charman/index.asp

Mary Cresswell is a science editor from Los Angeles. She lives in Kapiti and has published in a variety of online and print journals. Her book of satiric verse, *Nearest and Dearest*, is to be published by Steele Roberts in 2009. More information: http://www.bookcouncil.org.nz/writers/cresswellmary.html

James Dignan is an English-born writer, artist, and musician living in Dunedin. His writing mainly consists of articles and reviews for the *Otago Daily Times*, but also includes songs, poems, and short stories. He has also had several solo exhibitions of his paintings. His website: http://www.grutness.co.nz

John Dolan taught English at Otago for 10 years, then moved to Canada, where he became a pauper. He is now living the demeaning and exhausting life of an aged freelance writer. It serves him right. His books include *Stuck Up* (1995), *People with Real Lives Don't Need Landscapes* (2003) and *Pleasant Hell* (2005).

Marilyn Duckworth is a Wellington writer. Her fifteenth novel, *Playing Friends*, came out in 2007. She has published one poetry collection, *Other Lovers' Children*. More information: http://www.bookcouncil.org.nz/writers/duckworth.html

David Eggleton lives in Dunedin. He is a poet and writer whose articles, reviews and essays appear on a regular basis in a variety of publications. He has published a number of books of fiction and non-fiction, and his most recent collection of poetry is *Fast Talker*, released by AUP in 2006.

Chris Else's sixth novel *Gith* was published in 2008. He lives in Wellington and runs two websites, http://www.elseware.co.nz and http://www.ventiak.com. Another Internet project is in the making.

Andrew Fagan is a New Zealand poet, singer, songwriter and sailor. His books include four slim volumes of poetry, the latest being *Overnight Downpour* (HeadworX, 2006) and the autobiography/sailing memoir *Swirly World* (HarperCollins, 2001). More information: http://en.wikipedia.org/wiki/Andrew_Fagan

A.R.D. Fairburn (1904-1957) worked as a journalist, script-writer, union secretary, and tutor in the English Department at the University of Auckland. A notable painter and fabric designer, he taught at the Elam School of Fine Arts for the last 11 years of his life. His *Collected Poems* was published posthumously in 1966 by Pegasus Press, Christchurch, New Zealand.

Cliff Fell lives near Motueka, in the South Island. *Beauty of the Badlands* (VUP, 2008) is his second collection of poems. More information: http://www.bookcouncil.org.nz/writers/fellcliff.html

Gary Forrester lives in Wellington. He is the author of two novels, a book of poetry, and many academic articles. His website is http://www.garyforrester.com

Janis Freegard is one of three poets featured in *AUP New Poets 3* (AUP, 2008). Her poetry and fiction have appeared in *Landfall*, *JAAM*, *Poetry NZ*, *The North* and elsewhere. She shares her Wellington home with an historian, a cat, several weta and various inflatable baby aliens. Her blog is at http://janisfreegard.wordpress.com

Robin Fry, born in 1932 in Palmerston North, comes from a background of theatre, broadcasting and journalism. She is a graduate of Victoria University of Wellington and the Royal Academy of Dramatic Art (London). Author of three poetry collections, *Weather Report* (Inkweed, 2001), *Daymoon* (HeadworX, 2005) and *Inside It* (ESAW, 2006), Robin Fry won the open section of the NZ Poetry Society's International Competition in 2001 and in 2008.

Ruth Gilbert lives in Motueka. She received an award of Officer of the New Zealand Order of Merit in 2002 for services to poetry. Her collection *The Sunlit Hour* (1955) has been recently reprinted along with a new selection of her poems, *Selected Poems, 1941–1998* through Original Books, Wellington.

David Gregory is a Christchurch-based poet and environmental planner. He is an editor for Sudden Valley Press and a member of the Canterbury Poets Collective. He is the co-editor, with Coral Atkinson, of *Land Very Fertile: Banks Peninsula poetry and prose* (Canterbury University Press, 2008).

Nic Hill is a New Zealand writer. This is his first published poem.

Kevin Ireland was born in Mt Albert, Auckland, and now lives in Devonport. His 17th book of poems, *How to Survive the Morning*, and his fifth novel, *The Jigsaw Chronicles*, were published in 2008. Among his other publications are two memoirs, a volume of short stories, a booklet *On Getting Old* and a discursive book on fishing, *How to Catch a Fish*.

Rob Jackaman, born in England, won a Commonwealth Scholarship to study in Auckland and subsequently remained in New Zealand, where he has been a lecturer and creative writing course convenor. He is a widely published poet.

Anna Jackson has published four solo collections of poetry, the most recent being *The Gas Leak* (AUP, 2006), and also *Locating the Madonna* (Seraph Press, 2004), a collaboration with Jenny Powell. She lectures in the Department of English at Victoria University of Wellington.

Louis Johnson (1924-88) was one of New Zealand's most widely admired poets and editors. A journalist, editor and teacher, Johnson founded the *New Zealand Poetry Yearbook* (1951-64) and was a prolific poet. After spending much of the '70s in Australia, Johnson returned to Wellington in 1980. His *Selected Poems*, edited by Terry Sturm, was published posthumously in 2000.

Tim Jones is a poet, short story writer and novelist. His most recent books are the short story collection *Transported* (Vintage, 2008), which was long-listed for the 2008 Frank O'Connor International Short Story Award; the poetry collection *All Blacks' Kitchen Gardens* (HeadworX, 2007); and the fantasy novel *Anarya's Secret* (RedBrick, 2007). More information: http://timjonesbooks. blogspot.com

David Kārena-Holmes is a Dunedin poet and linguist. His poetry includes the long poem *From the Antipodes*, an extract of which was published by Maungatua Press in 2002, with a new edition in 2003.

Phil Kawana, Ngāruahine, Ngāti Ruanui and Ngāti Kahungunu, lives in Wellington, New Zealand. He has had poems published widely in anthologies and journals. He has published several books of poetry and fiction, including *Dead Jazz Guys* and *Attack of the Skunk People* (Huia Publishers, 1996 and 1999 respectively) and *Devil in my Shoes* (AUP, 2005).

Fiona Kidman (DCNZM), born in 1940, is best known for her novels, which include *A Breed of Women* and *The Book of Secrets*. Kidman has also written plays and poetry. Her selected poems, *Wakeful Nights*, was published in 1991. More recently she has edited *New Zealand Love Stories* for OUP and *Best New Zealand Fiction* for Vintage. A memoir, *At the End of Darwin Road*, was published in 2008.

Hilaire Kirkland (1941-1975) was a New Zealand poet. Her collection *Blood Clear and Apple Red* was published by Wai-te-ata Press, Wellington, in 1981.

Katherine Liddy recently published one-third of *AUP New Poets 3* and is now working on 'A Bee on His Lips', a series of poems set in ancient Greece. She lives and writes in Vancouver, Canada. Her blog: http://katherineliddy.blogspot.com

Rachel McAlpine is a poet, blogger, novelist, playwright and adviser on writing content for web sites. Her *Selected Poems* appeared from Mallinson Rendel in 1988, and her most recent novel is *Humming* (Hazard Press, 2005). More information: http://www.bookcouncil.org.nz/writers/mcalpiner.html, and http://www.writing.co.nz/

Tracie McBride is a New Zealander who lives in Melbourne with her family. Her work has appeared in over 40 publications, including *Pulp.Net*, *JAAM*, *Abyss and Apex*, *Space & Time*, *Sniplits* and *Electric Velocipede*. She won the Sir Julius Vogel Award for Best New Talent for 2007.

Seán McMahon is a New Zealand poet and author of several experimental chapbooks. His work has been published in *JAAM* and other journals.

Harvey McQueen has published six volumes of poetry. The latest, published by HeadworX, are *Pingandy* (1999) and *Recessional* (2004). Born in Little River, he grew up on Banks Peninsula, and worked in education until his retirement in 2002. He is well-known as an anthologist and was co-editor of the *Penguin Book of New Zealand Verse*. His latest is a selection of garden poems.

Owen Marshall has written or edited 23 books, including a collection of poetry. He received the ONZM for services to literature, and an honorary Doctorate of Letters from the University of Canterbury, where he is an adjunct professor. He has a particular affinity for rural and provincial life. More information: http://www.bookcouncil.org.nz/writers/marshallo.html

Jane Matheson is a guitarist, songwriter and poet. Her last performance was at The Adelaide, Wellington in 2007. Her recorded works to date are *To Aotearoa with Love* (solo debut album, 2003) and *Peace Wish* (a short poetry-play, 1998). She is currently working on a collection of new songs and can be contacted at imagine2nzaotearoa@hotmail.com

Thomas Mitchell is an Auckland-based writer. His book reviews, poetry and short stories have appeared in publications such as *Trout*, *JAAM*, *Evasion*, the *Dominion Post* and several editions of *New Zealand Short Short Stories*. This is his first published science fiction.

Harvey Molloy lives in Wellington where he teaches at Newlands College. His poems have appeared in *Albatross*, *Blackmail Press*, *Bravado*, *JAAM*, *New Zealand Listener*, *Poetry NZ*, *Southern Ocean Review* and *Takahe*. His first book of poems is *Moonshot* (Steele Roberts, 2008). More information: http://harveymolloy.blogspot.com

Michael Morrissey has published 19 books – 10 books of poetry, four of fiction and edited five anthologies of poetry and prose. He was the first writer-in-residence at the University of Canterbury in 1979 and the first New Zealand writer to participate in the University of Iowa's International Writing Programme. He has been writing a book review column for *Investigate* magazine for ten years during which time he has reviewed some 500 books.

James Norcliffe has published six collections of poetry, most recently *Along Blueskin Road* (Canterbury University Press, 2005) and *Villon in Millerton* (AUP, 2007). He has also published six novels for younger people, most recently *The Assassin of Gleam* (winner of the Sir Julius Vogel Award) and *The Loblolly Boy* (Longacre), and a collection of short stories, *The Chinese Interpreter*.

Michael O'Leary is a poet, novelist, artist, performer and bookshop/art gallery proprietor. O'Leary's career as a literary publisher covers twenty years. He has worked under two main imprints: The Earl of Seacliff Art Workshop (ESAW) and Miracle Mart Receiving. Web address: http://www.earlofseacliff.co.nz. His novels include *Unlevel Crossings*, *Out of It* and *Straight*. His poetry is collected in three volumes from HeadworX: *Toku Tinihanga: Selected Poems 1982-2002*, *Make Love and War* and *Paneta Street*.

Stephen Oliver's latest collection of poetry is *Harmonic* (Interactive Publications, 2008): see http://ipoz.biz/Titles/HAR.htm. IP also released the *King Hit* CD – poems written and read by Oliver to music composed by Matt Ottley – in 2007.

Jacqueline Crompton Ottaway has had poetry, stories, articles and books published in New Zealand and overseas. She belongs to several poetry and writing groups and enjoys sharing her work with friends and colleagues. Jacqueline is often surprised how memories, dreams and reflections are echoed in her poems.

Alistair Paterson (ONZM) is a poet, editor, anthologist, fiction writer and critic. In addition to his own work, such as his recent collections *Summer on the Côte d'Azur* (HeadworX, 2003), and the long poem *Africa* (Puriri Press, 2008), he has made a notable contribution to New Zealand poetry as editor of *Climate* and *Poetry NZ* (http://www.poetrynz.net/). More information: http://www.bookcouncil.org.nz/writers/patersona.html

Jack Perkins runs the Spectrum radio documentary unit in Radio New Zealand, and is also a cricketer, writer and blogger. A collection of his cricket blogs, *Not Out! No Ball! Over!*, has just been published.

Chris Pigott has been published in various New Zealand anthologies and journals, such as *The NeXt Wave*, *Sport*, and *JAAM*. He is currently living in Thailand.

Mark Pirie is a Wellingon writer and the publisher for HeadworX (http://headworx.eyesis.co.nz). He initiated, co-founded and edited *JAAM* magazine (1995-2005) and currently edits *broadsheet: new new zealand poetry*. His books include *Gallery* (poetry, Salt Publishing, UK) and the anthology, *The NeXt Wave* (University of Otago Press). More information: http://www.bookcouncil.org.nz/writers/piriemark.html

Vivienne Plumb is an award-winning playwright, poet and fiction writer. She has held the NZ Buddle Findlay Sargeson Fellowship. Her new play, *The Wife Who Spoke Japanese In Her Sleep*, will premiere at the 2009 Auckland Festival. More information: http://www.bookcouncil.org.nz/writers/plumbviv.html

Jenny Powell is a Dunedin writer who has published three individual and two collaborative collections of poems. Her next collection, *Viet Nam: a poem journey* is to be published by HeadworX.

Born in New Zealand, **Cath Randle** had her first poem published at 18 and first science fiction short story at 28. An English émigré, she gained an MA in Creative and Critical Writing at Winchester University in 2008. She lives in Hampshire with her family. For more information: http://twitter.com/CathodeRandle

Trevor Reeves lives and writes in Dunedin. Former publisher and editor of *Southern Ocean Review*, writer of eight books including short stories, poetry, non-fiction including books on dams, crime, etc. His work has been published worldwide: poems, short stories, reviews, non-fiction etc. More information: http://www.book.co.nz

Helen Rickerby's most recent book of poetry, *My Iron Spine*, was published in 2008 by HeadworX. She is co-managing editor of *JAAM* literary magazine, and runs the small publishing company, Seraph Press. She can often be found at http://wingedink.blogspot.com

Anna Rugis is a former backup singer for Van Morrison, Cat Stevens, The Kinks, Cliff Richard and others. Her CDs include *Reconciliation, Cave Songs*, and *Traffic in Gold*. She also writes musicals for schools on environmental themes, including *Island Dreams, Home Free*, and *River Songs*. More information: http://www.myspace.com/annarugis

Bill Sewell (1951-2003) was a New Zealand poet, editor, anthologist and reviewer, whose collections include *Solo Flight* (University of Otago Press, 1982), *Erebus* (Hazard Press, 1999), and *The Ballad of Fifty-one* (HeadworX, 2003). He was posthumously awarded the inaugural Lauris Edmond Memorial Award for Poetry in 2003. More information: http://www.bookcouncil.org.nz/writers/sewellbill.html

Iain Sharp was born, like *Fahrenheit 451*, in the year 1953, but in defiance of Ray Bradbury's dystopian vision he has spent much of his working life as a librarian. He is the author of four volumes of poetry. His most recent publication is an illustrated biography of Nineteenth-Century artist and explorer Charles Heaphy.

Meliors Simms is a Canadian-born, New Zealand-raised, well travelled sci-fi reader. Gripped by a mid-life fever of creativity that doggedly distracts her from taking gainful employment seriously, if she's not busy writing she's busy making things (like books). Her peripatetic, literary and artistic pursuits are documented in *Bibliophilia*, the blog she's proud to have been posting since 2005: http://www.meliors.net/

Robert Sullivan, Ngā Puhi, is a poet, editor, anthologist, librarian and creative writing teacher. He was a co-editor of *Whetu Moana: Contemporary Polynesian Poems in English* (AUP, 2003), the first anthology of contemporary indigenous Polynesian poetry in English edited by Polynesians. His poetry collections include *Star Waka* (1999) and *Captain Cook in the Underworld* (2002). More information: http://www.bookcouncil.org.nz/writers/sullivanrobert.html

Brian Turner is an Otago poet, essayist and biographer whose works include the biography of Colin Meads, *Meads* (Hodder Moa Beckett, 2006); poetry collections including *Footfall* (Godwit, 2005), arising from his tenure as the Te Mata Estate Poet Laureate; and *Into the Wider World: A back country miscellany* (Godwit, 2008), a collection of essays, columns, articles and poetry. More information: http://www.bookcouncil.org.nz/writers/turnerbrian.html

Tze Ming Mok is a poet, fiction writer and essayist whose work has been published in *Landfall, Sport, Poetry NZ, Meanjin, JAAM* and *New Zealand Listener*. Her poem 'An Arabic Poetry Lesson in Jakarta' was selected as one of the *Best New Zealand Poems 2004*. More information: http://www.bookcouncil.org.nz/writers/moktzeming.html

Richard von Sturmer is an Auckland writer and filmmaker. His most recent book, *Suchness: Zen Poetry and Prose*, was published by HeadworX in 2005. As far as Science Fiction goes, he is a fan of Stanislaw Lem and Boris and Arkady Strugatsky. For more, see http://www.bookcouncil.org.nz/writers/vonsturmerrichard.html

Nelson Wattie is a Wellington poet, book reviewer and translator. He is co-editor of the *Oxford Companion to New Zealand Literature*, with Roger Robinson.

Mike Webber's poetry is performance and comedy oriented. And sci-fi has always (since he began reading!) been one of his loves, the others being music, doing sport, driving, nature, women, love and sex! Known as 'Mike Tights' (after his poetry uniform) he has been writing and performing poetry for 20+ years.

Simon Williamson (1968-1999) was born in Ngaruawahia, New Zealand. Published in literary magazines like *JAAM* and *Takahe*, he sang in the folk bands, The Flat Earthers and Between Earth and Sky. His posthumous book, *Storyteller: Poems 1988-1999* (HeadworX, 2002), was widely acclaimed and his poems continue to find publication in anthologies and journals.

Sue Wootton is a Dunedin poet and short fiction writer. Her published poetry collections are *Hourglass* (Steele Roberts, 2005) and *Magnetic South* (Steele Roberts, 2008). She has won prizes and commendations in various competitions, including a place in the 2008 NZ Book Month Six Pack 3 competition with her short story 'Virtuoso'. She was the 2008 Robert Burns Fellow at Otago University in 2008, and was a finalist in the 2008 *Sunday Star Times* short story competition with a tale called 'Beyond Pluto'. More information: http://www.bookcouncil.org.nz/writers/woottonsue.html

Recent IP Poetry

Liquefaction, Iain Britton
ISBN 9781921479175, AU$25 / NZ$28.95

in between the dancing, E A Gleeson
ISBN 9781921479106, AU$25 / NZ$28.95

Invaders of the Heart, Lee Knowles
ISBN 9781921479090, AU$25 / NZ$28.95

the possibility of flight, Lia Hills
ISBN 9781921479076, AU$25 / NZ$28.95

Death and the Motorway, David Gilbey
ISBN 9781876819781, AU$25 / NZ$28.95

Harmonic, Stephen Oliver
ISBN 9781876819743, AU$25 / NZ$28.95

Straggling Into Winter, Kathy Kituai
ISBN 9781876819699, AU$24 / NZ$27.95

Someone Forgot to Tell the Fish, Hal Judge
ISBN 9781876819712, AU$24 / NZ$27.95

What Can Be Proven, Mark O'Flynn
ISBN 9781876819669, AU$24 / NZ$27.95

With One Brush, Jan Dean
ISBN 9781876819675, AU$24 / NZ$27.95

For the latest from IP, please visit us online at
http://ipoz.biz/Store/Store.htm
*or contact us by **phone/fax** at 61 7 3324 9319 or 61 7 3395 0269*
or sales@ipoz.biz